30-DAY MENTAL DIET

30-DAY
MENTAL
DIET

THE WAY TO
A BETTER LIFE

WILLIS KINNEAR

SCIENCE OF MIND PUBLICATIONS
Los Angeles, California

Fourteenth Printing - August 1984

Published by SCIENCE OF MIND PUBLICATIONS
3251 West Sixth Street, Los Angeles, California 90020

Copyright © 1963 by Science of Mind Publications
ISBN 0-911336-20-6

CONTENTS

THIRD WEEK

FOURTH WEEK

SUMMARY

INTRODUCTION

Why any kind of diet, let alone a mental diet?

Usually a diet refers to food, the amount and kind that we eat. The elements of the diet are carefully selected so as to accomplish certain desired results. Food diets may be for the purpose of losing weight, gaining weight, or to provide a more balanced intake of food to create a better condition and tone of the body. Then there are those diets which are for the purpose of correcting or alleviating some bodily condition which is other than normal.

When adhered to consistently, such diets usually accomplish the desired results. The person feels better, looks better, and is much happier.

So why not have a mental diet? We are constantly filling our minds with thoughts of all kinds. Little selection is done. It seems that the mind is a giant hopper into which all manner of things are dumped with little concern as to what happens afterward. Yet it is the mind, and its content of thought, which determines to a large degree the functioning and health of our physical bodies, the state of our relationships with others, and the degree of success which we may be able to achieve.

Perhaps if we would embark on a regime of mental dieting, carefully watching what enters into and is entertained in thought, selecting specific types of thought for certain specific results, barring other thoughts which are definitely productive of results other than those which we desire, then we might be able to make more of ourselves than we now are and enjoy a richer, fuller life. Controlled diet, either of food or thought, cannot help but result in control of what we experience.

So try a mental diet for thirty days. It can be fun, interesting, and very productive. While on the mental diet numerous ideas will be encountered which may be somewhat new. But they are ideas whose nutritious value and productivity of results have been proved.

One paramount requirement of any diet is that it is followed through to the end, and that there is no variation in its content. It is only by following all instructions carefully that results are achieved.

What results are desired from a mental diet? Just name them—a greater degree of health, happiness, or success—a mental diet can give them to you.

STOP

Before starting your thirty-day mental diet read these instructions carefully and follow them without fail. This is not material to be read all at once; instead, it is a sequence of ideas to be read and used *one each day*. The value to be gained from any thirty-day program cannot be achieved by doing everything in one day. The ideas you will find here might be compared to a bottle of vitamins; if you are supposed to take one a day, which is all you can absorb, then it would be useless to gulp them all at one time. To get the most benefit follow the instructions.

INSTRUCTIONS

Establish a definite program for yourself. The mental diet for each day requires about six minutes to read. There is a space for you to note the date and time that it is read; also a place to note the time that it is *reread*. It is suggested that the first reading be in the morning and the second at night.

Each mental diet consists of four basic parts. First there is the presentation of the idea and an explanation of its nature and sphere of influence. This is followed by "Mental Stimulants" for the day—words of the great and the wise which confirm the authenticity of the idea for the day. Then "The Diet" itself, which enables you to apply the idea for the day in a practical manner in relation to your health, affairs, and relationships. The *diet* is mental food. Assimilate it, make it part of yourself, mentally and emotionally, and it will nourish and sustain you. And finally there is a "Capsule Supplement" which is easily assimilated and remembered.

30-DAY MENTAL DIET

A word of caution: No diet will work unless you follow it faithfully. First, there is the necessity of using the diet each day in the manner suggested. Second, the diet will have little value for you if you counteract it in between readings by dumping into your mind ideas which are contrary to it. Don't let yourself slip in this manner. If you find you are doing so, immediately reread or recall the diet, regardless of the place or time. Don't waver in your intent; don't deprive yourself of the benefits that you can receive from it.

As for the wording of the diet, it may or may not be flavored to suit you. If you desire, rephrase the idea in your own words—it is the idea that is important.

The effectiveness of the 30-Day Mental Diet need not be questioned. Of course an inquiring mind will have certain doubts about any new idea; however, those you will encounter here have been tested and proved, not only today but down through the ages. They are universal truths to be discovered and used. They exist to be used, but their proper use is up to you. There are certain things others can do for you, but there is one thing that only you can do for yourself—*think*—and think in a manner so that your thoughts will have a salutary effect on your daily living.

THE
FIRST
WEEK

During the first seven days ideas are presented which are fundamental to every aspect of your life. They will help you to clarify your thoughts about many questions every person asks himself, and which need to be answered before you can find security and your proper place in the scheme of things.

WHO YOU ARE · WHERE YOU ARE · WHY YOU ARE IMPORTANT

LEARN TO THINK CONSTRUCTIVELY · LIFE IS FOR YOU

YOU HAVE GREAT POSSIBILITIES · DISCOVERING YOURSELF

WHO YOU ARE

You Are More Than You Think You Are

Have you ever taken time to really think about yourself? With the pressure and demands of present-day living it may have been a little difficult, but perhaps at some time or other there has been a chance to *think* and no doubt the questions have arisen in your mind as to just *who* and *what* you are. Puzzling questions to say the least, but ones demanding a satisfactory answer if you are to avoid the feeling of a gnawing problem. And nothing is to be gained by pushing the questions back into the limbo of the unconscious mind where they still will be demanding answers whether you acknowledge it or not.

Appearances Are Misleading

When you got up this morning and looked in the mirror, what did you see? Very likely it was not too pleasant a sight but nevertheless there you were, or what you thought you were. Eyes, ears, nose, mouth, hair. Was that *you?* After you were dressed and entered into your day's activities your family, friends, and associates could see you. Was what they saw *you?* What they saw and recognized was what they knew to be you, but was it *really* you?

Just What Are You?

You know yourself as possessing a body. You know yourself as having certain emotional reactions. You know yourself as thinking in a certain way. But the *real* you which has a body, which has feelings, which thinks—what is it?

Some time ago, when prices were lower, it was determined that your body was composed of water and about ninety-eight cents worth of chemicals. Is that what you would

WHO YOU ARE

say you are? Common sense would dictate that you are much, much more than can be determined in the chemical laboratory.

You have emotions. You get hungry, you get cold, you get hot. You have feelings of love, hate, anger, anxiety, fear, and joy. These emotions could not be what you are, for you experience them. What is it that experiences them?

The Brain a Machine

You think, or at least most people like to think that they think. What is it that does the thinking? The brain seems to be the part of the body in which thought resides, or is the channel for it. Physiology has never found a brain that could think by itself. The brain, with its billions of interconnecting nerves, appears to be nothing more or less than a colossal computing machine. Such electronic machines are fast, accurate, and amazingly able. But electronic engineers have no hope that one will ever be able *to think*. The brain, like the electronic computor, is also a machine. Neither can write Shakespeare's plays, paint Michelangelo's pictures, nor thrill to a sunset. There has to be a *thinker* behind them.

It would appear that that which you really are is that *something* which *thinks, something* which has a body, which feels and has emotions, and which is aware of itself through the process of thought.

The Mystery of Mind

Now that you have made yourself out to be *something* which thinks and is self-conscious—mind—the problem arises as to where did it come from? Is it compounded of the chemicals that comprise the body? Mix chemicals together as long as you want but will you ever be able to make them think? Mind, nebulous and ethereal as it may seem, appears to be the ultimate thing you are, yet it cannot appear out of the nowhere. Mind is definitely something, intangible as it is.

You are, in essence, mind, and it would stand to reason that you could not have

WHO YOU ARE

created yourself or else you would be able to create yourself time and time again.

So to find out what you really are you have to determine what mind is.

Where Do You Come From?

It appears that there must be something in the universe that is intelligent, that is capable of conscious thought. Since every man thinks, and since the universe is a unity and not a chaos or divided against itself, there must be a single source of the *thinker* that each man is. It appears that there would have to be, and must be, an infinite Thinker or Mind which expresses in and through each person as that person.

You, as an individual, are a conscious intelligent thinker. And your mind is, and could only be, an individualization of the One Mind and Intelligence. This Mind is at once both infinite and particularized as your mind.

MENTAL STIMULANTS

SCIENCE: *The important point is that man's spirit, certainly an inhabitant of his living, material body, may without philosophical impropriety be regarded as similar in nature to a far greater Spirit, in which thus, literally, he may be said to live and move and have his being.*

—Edmund W. Sinnott

PHILOSOPHY: *We, each of us, are a distinct part of the essence of God and contain a certain part of Him in ourselves.*

—Epictetus

RELIGION: *Know ye not that ye are the temple of God, and that the Spirit of God dwelleth in you?*

—I Corinthians 3:16

WHO YOU ARE

THE DIET

Today I identify myself with That which is greater than I am, which is both the source of what I am and is what I am. The One infinite Mind, Intelligence, Spirit—God —that created all things and is all things, is also in me as me. I know that my body is an expression of Its infinite creativity; that my mind, my self-conscious ability to think, that which I know as my *real* self, is an individualization of the infinite Mind of God as my mind. I now recognize the *real* me for all that it is—an expression and conscious activity of the Mind of God, infinite Consciousness. I am that which It is, It is that which I am. Each day I become increasingly aware that God is what I am. I affirm the reality of that Power greater than I am, and as I do so with complete faith, belief, and conviction in It, and identify myself with It, I accept and permit It to flow into ever fuller expression as what I am. The One Mind, One Life, God, with infinite power and creativity for good in all things, today finds an unhindered channel for increased expression as me.

—Capsule Supplement—

There is only One Mind, Spirit, or Intelligence which increasingly flows into fuller harmonious expression as all that I am. As I now affirm this, and accept it, so it is done.

✿　✿　✿

Today I will apply this idea to these aspects of my thoughts and actions:

_____

_____

My particular problem, condition, or situation which it can be used to correct is:

_____

_____

WHERE YOU ARE

You Are in the Midst of the Universe

Perhaps you know exactly where you are, or rather you think you know. You know you live in a certain house, on a certain street, in a certain state of a particular country. But, on the other hand, you are one of several billions of people occupying the land portion of the earth. And the land occupies only a small part of the earth's surface, about one-third.

The earth itself? A relatively small planet, one of nine major ones revolving around a rather small star—our sun. Our sun-star, one of billions, is located near the edge of a spiral stellar galaxy—we see a portion of it at night as the Milky Way—which is not too impressive in a universe containing countless such galaxies. And the astronomers say that of the limitless numbers of stars in the universe many have planets about them that could have some sort of life on them.

In spite of the appearance of your relatively insignificant position in the scheme of things, do not start to belittle yourself yet.

The Stars Are Your Relatives

Your body is made up of the food you eat, the water you drink, and the air you breathe. It might be said that it is built out of the elements of the earth itself. And what of them? They are the same fundamental elements out of which the sun and the farthest star are composed. The stuff of your body and the twinkling star you see in the night sky are basically comprised of the same materials. You are a part of the universe, of all creation, which is so vast man has not yet even started to comprehend its full nature.

WHERE YOU ARE

Cosmic Drama

You are part of the great cosmic drama. You are not separate from but part of all that you can see. And where you are, from the viewpoint of the cosmos, is just as important as any other part, for it is composed of the same materials as any other part.

The dynamic creative quality, which may also be designated as the Direction, Purpose, Consciousness, or Intelligence, evident in operation throughout the cosmos is also functioning right where you are. Its action there is just as complete as it is in the island universes so distant as to be barely discernible.

Where you are is a focal point of the great infinite cosmic drama that is forever unfolding, which indicates a purposiveness and design, and law and order in everything.

Nothing Lacking

Inherent where you are are all the fundamental materials of the physical universe, all the intelligence, purpose, and creative power that exist anywhere. The main point is that you need to become aware of this and realize that where you are is part of all that is. As much as you might try, you cannot cut yourself off nor isolate yourself from the Creativity of the universe which is intelligent, orderly, and definite. And this Creativity could never be chaotic or in conflict with Itself, or the universe would destroy itself.

So you find that fundamentally there is nothing lacking where you are. The harmonious creative action of the universe is available right where you are—all of it, not just part of it. The same basic building blocks out of which all things are made surround you and are within you and function according to the same law and order that holds the planets in their places.

Where you are is included in the great scheme of things which man is dimly beginning to understand. Insignificant as where you are may seem, all the elements of the universe are available there, and most important of all, the great Creativity that exists everywhere is in no respect diminished there.

WHERE YOU ARE

Limitless Possibilities

This is a wonderful concept once you are able to grasp its full value and meaning. For you have available for your use all that is—all the power, law, and elements out of which everything is created. Where you are is the most important place in the cosmos, for all of its creative action is available in and at that particular place. Your responsibility is in *knowing* this and in the use of this knowledge in what you do.

MENTAL STIMULANTS

SCIENCE: *Through the new point of view of science, we realize that we are not material things, that we are composed of this complex harmony of atomic matter, and through the mysteries of this great harmony within us we are linked to each other and to the harmony of the spheres—the harmony of creation. In the pattern of these relationships we see how there can be a Creator of the universe who can hold in His hand the farthest reaches of the stars and at the same time stand close by each of us, ready to strengthen and sustain us if we turn to Him.*

—Donald Hatch Andrews

PHILOSOPHY: *There is one mind common to all individual men. Every man is an inlet to the same and to all of the same...Who hath access to this universal mind is a party to all that is or can be done, for this is the only sovereign agent.*

—Ralph Waldo Emerson

RELIGION: *And there are diversities of operations, but it is the same God which worketh all in all.*

—I Corinthians 12:6

WHERE YOU ARE

THE DIET

I am not alone. I belong to Life and all of Life. All that Life is is right where I am and is what I am. There is no separation. I am an individualization of that greater Whole, the nature and purposefulness of which are fully present at every point within It. Not part of God, not part of Life, not part of the universal Creativity, but all of It is available right where I am and as what I am. I no longer separate myself from Life, but recognize and identify myself with It. The infinite potentiality and possibility of every good thing is immediately available to me right now, right where I am. The substance of all things, the immutable action of all law, the conscious activity of the One Mind are all present and available here and now. I know and declare that every aspect of my life and experience today and every day continues to become a more perfect expression and harmonious manifestation of the nature of the One Mind—God—which can only be good.

—Capsule Supplement—

All of Life, God, is active right where I am, right now. I discard all previous ideas of separation. As I consciously unite myself with God, the limitless possibilities of every good thing become available in my life.

o o o

Today I will apply this idea to these aspects of my thoughts and actions:

_____

_____

My particular problem, condition, or situation which it can be used to correct is:

_____

_____

WHY YOU ARE IMPORTANT

You Are Necessary to Life

When you examine yourself you discover that you are probably somewhere between five and six feet tall. You find that you are neither very big nor very small as things appear in your world. If you were able to envision the size of a star and also that of an atom, you would be able to determine that in relation to size you are just about in the middle of things. All of which leaves you in the position of not being very impressive one way or the other as far as size is concerned.

So in what respect are you able to discover that you may have any importance?

You are Unique

To begin with, there is no one else just like you. There never has been and there never will be another *you*. Nature never duplicates itself. Everything is a unique and individual expression of Life. Life is expressing Itself in and through you in a way that is a one-time-only creation.

Inasmuch as there is always a purposive drive in every living thing, this would mean that in you there is a coming forth of Life that seeks to express and create in a manner that will never be duplicated. You are important in the scheme of things for Life seeks to be in and through *you* what It has never been before. Your mind, your consciousness, is a particular channel for the flowing into expression of the One Mind, the One Intelligence that is the heart of the universe.

WHY YOU ARE IMPORTANT

Your Need To Create

"So what?" you may ask. "Why should I concern myself with such things?"

Life should be lived and enjoyed. It holds infinite possibilities for enjoyment, happiness, and accomplishment; but only if you stop vegetating, just existing, and give full expression to the greater potentialities that reside within you.

You need to become aware of what you are, where you are, and your importance as a unique creation of and channel for the flow of the One Mind into individual expression. It needs you for fulfillment of Its creativity and Its flowing into individuality. And you need to recognize It as what you are and come to assist Its flow in and as you, rather than blocking Its action through indifference and lack of knowledge.

You are the most important person in the world. This is not conceit, for every other person is also the most important person. Each and every one has his own particular place to fulfill in the limitless variety of expressions of the Infinite.

You Have a Job To Do

No one else can live the life you are living. No one else can bring into tangible experience the creative activity of Mind the way you can. You are unique. You are a one-and-only expression of God. You are important to yourself and to Life for no one else can creatively express Life the way you can.

You must come to value your place in the greater scheme of things. You must ever seek to discover the best that is within you and never cease to express to the fullest your creative ability in every respect. The best you do will always be a far cry from the best you can do, for there is a limitless potential of ability that is always trying to find its way into expression through you.

Live Up to Your Importance

You are important. Live up to that importance. You have an obligation to Life. Assume your responsibility of importance. It is then, and only then, that you will become the greater person you can be.

WHY YOU ARE IMPORTANT

But do not misinterpret the meaning of the word importance. It does not necessarily mean that you must be a "very important person" to the newspapers, nor famous for certain achievements. It does mean that you must become a more complete channel for the expression of the things that really count in life, even though right now they may not extend beyond your family circle. To really be an important individualization of Life you must in all you do express love, harmony, and creativity, for the greatest possible good for yourself and others. In doing this you open up the way to becoming of greater importance and value to Life, to yourself, and to your fellow man.

MENTAL STIMULANTS

SCIENCE: *...while the Great Architect had to direct alone the earlier stages of the evolutionary process, that part of Him that becomes us*—for we are certainly inside, not outside, Creation's plan—*has been stepping up amazingly the* pace *of vegetable, animal, and human evolution since we began to become conscious of the part we had to play.* It is our sense of responsibility for playing our part to the best of our ability that makes us Godlike.

—Robert A. Millikan

PHILOSOPHY: *No individual, however great, can be an exhaustive expression of God but each individual is a distinctive expression and brings out a characteristic of God's being. It may be said that every human being is unique and answers to a specific need in God.*

—Sarvepalli Radhakrishnan

RELIGION: *For the Father loveth the Son, and sheweth him all things that himself doeth: and he will shew him greater works than these, that ye may marvel.*

—John 5:20

WHY YOU ARE IMPORTANT

THE DIET

Without any sense of conceit or false idea of importance I know that I am a unique creation of God. Never before and never again will there ever be another *me*. God goes forth anew into creation as what I am. I accept my unique individuality and recognize my responsibility to more fully express the Life that is within me. With a certainty that it is done, I declare that there are now removed all ideas and emotional responses which may have prevented the fullness of Life from expressing in and through me. I fulfill my obligation to Life in every respect. I let It be all that It is at Its level of expression as me. I now declare that I become a fuller channel for Its continual creative action for good in every aspect of my life and experience. I accept and constantly endeavor to more fully express the unique individualization of God in me and know that in so doing, through God's eternal creative action, I am rightly guided in all that I do. I am important to God and important to myself, for I know that God continues to create and express in and through everything I do. In this knowledge my life now becomes a joyous adventure and a continually fuller attainment of what I know my true nature to be.

—Capsule Supplement—

I am important, a unique individualization of God. Through this awareness Life now finds a freer, fuller channel for the expression of Its perfect nature as me.

✿ ✿ ✿

Today I will apply this idea to these aspects of my thoughts and actions:

_____

_____

My particular problem, condition, or situation which it can be used to correct is:

_____

_____

LEARN TO THINK CONSTRUCTIVELY

It Is Necessary that You Think in a Constructive Manner

Now that you have some idea as to who you are, where you are, and the importance of yourself, the question arises as to the nature of the creative activity of your mind.

You have ascertained that you are essentially mind, consciousness—an intelligent thinker. And this is also the nature of the creative Power back of the universe. Pure thought in the Mind of God, infinite Intelligence, is the one and only source of all things. A thought in Mind manifests itself in and as the physical universe in accord with the law and order of its own nature.

Think Carefully

Similarly, inasmuch as your mind is an expression and activity of the One Mind, it would stand to reason that it is also creative. Creative not on a cosmic scale, but in your own life and experience. Your thinking determines your experience. In fact your thoughts *become* the conditions and situations you encounter in daily living.

If you find yourself prone to argue with this idea, relax for a while. The proof of the pudding is in the eating. The time will come when you will prove for yourself the validity of this concept. In the meantime accept it at face value. Proceed on the assumption that it is true. Others have proved this true and there is no reason why you cannot prove it true for yourself.

LEARN TO THINK CONSTRUCTIVELY

Thoughts Are Things

Thoughts become your experiences.

The activity of Life is a constructive process. It is forever building things up, creating and organizing in a purposive manner in accord with some design. The purpose and the design discernible in all that lives are not to be found in the chemical elements comprising any living thing. The purpose and design or pattern are nebulous and intangible. Yet they are the causative factors. They are intelligent. They act in accord with law. They evidence order and harmonious creativity. They could have only one source—conscious Intelligence, Life, Mind, God.

But a problem arises: If it is the nature of Mind to be constructive and creative as the result of the process of Its thought, how constructive and beneficial is *your* creative thought? It is creative by nature, but how about the constructive aspect? By constructive is meant, is it *beneficially* creative? Does it produce a better life and experience for you? Think this over carefully. To what extent is your thinking positive or negative, constructive or destructive, beneficial or detrimental? In other words, just what are you doing to yourself?

Thinking Can Be Harmful

Infinite Mind could never think in a destructive manner or It would destroy Itself. But you have been created free to think as you choose. You may think in any manner you so desire, either in accord with the nature of the constructive beneficial thought of the One Mind, or destructively in any way you may care to. And man seems to have thought up many unique patterns of negative thinking!

Once you fully realize the creative nature of your thought you will know that the consistent pattern of your thinking is what you are experiencing in your health, affairs, and relationships. What do you want life to be for you? What it becomes starts with the way you think. Just how costly are some of your thought patterns? Can you afford them?

LEARN TO THINK CONSTRUCTIVELY

Constructive Thinking

One of the purposes of this mental diet is to get you started thinking in a constructive manner. Creating good in your life and experience rather than just wishing things were better and thinking constantly about how bad they are.

Clear, consistent, affirmative patterns of thought will be creative of a fuller, richer life. It is yours for the thinking and for the carrying of the thought into action in your daily living.

You can start to do this now. You do not need to wait for something big to come along, some crisis or perplexing problem. You think all the time, you are doing things all the time. Tie the two together right now. There is nothing big or little to the creative power of thought, but once you realize it works in the so-called little things of life you will have no misgivings about its power in relation to the solutions of problems which seem big to you.

MENTAL STIMULANTS

SCIENCE: *We discover that the universe shows evidence of a designing or controlling power that has something in common with our own individual minds.*

—Sir James Jeans

PHILOSOPHY: *The thoughts of the Soul are not ideas but creative powers...the more the Soul lives in the light of the Spirit, "turned towards" that which is above itself, the more creative it becomes.*

—Plotinus

RELIGION: *For it is not ye that speak, but the Spirit of your Father which speaketh in you.*

—Matthew 10:20

LEARN TO THINK CONSTRUCTIVELY

THE DIET

"For he [God] spake, and it was done." The creative Power of the conscious thought of infinite Mind, God, is the invisible source of all that is. This same creative Power resides in my thought and I may consciously direct It to the degree I am aware of It; it could not be otherwise. I speak my word and it is done. The words I speak, the thoughts I think, I know to be creative of my life and experience. In this knowledge rests my new-found key to a fuller enjoyment of all of Life's abundant riches. My thought is always creative and I now declare that my patterns of thinking will be of a constructive nature. I discard all tendencies to think in ways that may have been productive of undesirable experiences. Regardless of appearances I entertain only ideas of good—fine health, abundant supply of all things, and harmonious activities and relationships. The creative nature of my thought now has only ideas of good to work on. I renew the content of my mind and thus renew the content of my experience of Life. I stand guard at the gateway of my mind and entertain only those ideas which I desire to have become tangibly manifested. God declares Himself anew and goes forth into manifestation through every beneficial word I speak.

—Capsule Supplement—

As I now renew the content of my mind with only good and constructive ideas, I know that my entire life is remade to conform with the nature of these ideas.

✿　✿　✿

Today I will apply this idea to these aspects of my thoughts and actions:

_____

_____

My particular problem, condition, or situation which it can be used to correct is:

_____

_____

LIFE IS FOR YOU

Live Life, Don't Fight It

There is one thing you can be most certain of, and that is that law in some form or other guides and governs every aspect of your experience just as it does everything else in the universe. Fundamentally, the universe operates as a unity, not a chaos, and the laws that establish and maintain this unity are not in conflict with one another.

The creative action of infinite Intelligence is explained in terms of Law, and the operation of this Law is of necessity in conformity with Its nature, not contrary to It. So you can come to discover that it does not matter what your experience may be, whether you are concerned with your health, success, affairs, or relationships, there is a Law of Mind at work. But the *way* It works in and through your experience you determine. Things just do not happen haphazardly, without any determining factor. There is always a cause and effect, an initial act of creativity and the manifest result.

You Cannot Escape Law

Perhaps you have been prone to think that law is operative in some things and not in others—that there is a law relative to the action of electricity but no law that applies to your relationships with others. Or that law may apply to the positions the planets hold around the sun, but law does not enter into the question as to whether you are sick or well.

Whether you fully recognize it or not, law functions in everything you are, do, and experience. There is no avoiding or escaping its action. But it must always be remembered that law is impersonal. It is never concerned about whether or not you recognize it, nor is it the least bit interested in how you use it.

LIFE IS FOR YOU

Life Withholds Nothing

This definitely indicates that there is nothing in the nature of things that is intrinsically against your welfare or well-being. There is nothing in the universe that decrees that you shall be sick, poor, or unhappy. It would be impossible for a universe that manifests through law and order to declare that one individual shall enjoy life and another not. Neither would it be possible for the creative Intelligence in and back of all things to give an abundance of all things to one part of Its creation and deprive another part.

So it would appear that if in any respect Life seems to be withholding something from you, it is not the result of the action of Life Itself, but the result of your relationship to Life. All of Life is available to you, but the question that arises is: How much of It are you availing yourself of?

The Universe Does Not Have Favorites

Any law, in any sphere of activity, improperly used will bring improper results. In the physical world scientists are able to avail themselves of the power of nature only when they are able to ascertain the laws of its action and properly use them. You are in much the same position. You have to discover for yourself the nature of the spiritual Law which governs your experiences in living, and then properly apply It.

Where previously you may have been using the action of the Law of Mind erratically, with the result that you felt you had to wage a solitary battle against the universe, you will find that the proper use of the creative power of your thought, and its immutable action through Law, will align your life in harmony with the beneficial nature of God.

Let Life Help You

When you properly understand this you will find that Life is for you; then you can avail yourself of all Its good in your life. You use the Law for your benefit. It is futile to battle against Its action; you direct Its action in the manner you desire.

LIFE IS FOR YOU

Your ability to direct this action resides in the nature of the God-given creative power of your own thought.

When you stop battling life, stop feeling that everything is against you, and become aware of the fact that the only thing against you is your own thinking, then you start to cooperate with the great Law of the universe and through a change in the pattern of your thinking you will be able to make your life a joyous adventure in which you will encounter only good.

Regardless of how much misdirection you may have given the Law in the past, it is never too late to start to use It in a new and better way. The Law knows only to act, to respond to your thought. Your every thought is the start of a new causative action which will become manifest in your experience. And the wonderful thing is that this new action can transform and transcend any present undesirable condition in your life.

MENTAL STIMULANTS

SCIENCE: *God may be subtle, but he is not malicious.*
—Albert Einstein

PHILOSOPHY: *...man is confronted by something spiritually greater than himself which, in contrast to human nature and to all other phenomena, is Absolute Reality. Man's goal is to seek communion with the Presence behind the phenomena, and to seek it with the aim of bringing his self into harmony with this Absolute Reality.*
—Arnold J. Toynbee

RELIGION: *And God saw every thing that he had made, and, behold, it was very good.*
Genesis 1:31

— 31 —

LIFE IS FOR YOU

THE DIET

Life is for me now and always; It created me for Itself. The creative activity of the universe is for me as I now come to realize that there is nothing against me except my own ignorance or misunderstanding of the nature of Reality. I cease trying to change God, to revise the Law of the universe. I stop battling life, conditions, and situations. I no longer attempt to change ultimate Reality and the way It works. With definiteness and consistency I ever seek to cooperate with the great Law of Life and to align myself with It. There is no god, devil, or evil that desires my downfall. I know that when things are other than they should be they could have occurred only through my misuse and misdirection of the Law of Mind. Life does not limit Itself; I cease limiting myself. I am no longer my own worst enemy, for I now let my thoughts rest clearly and definitely on the fact that God is good, that my life is filled only with good as I mentally accept it in my experience. All limitations and barriers are removed as I now avail myself of the infinite creative power of Mind—the creative power of my thought—to make my experiences in life all that I desire them to be.

—Capsule Supplement—

I now release all ideas and concepts that are detrimental to my good and replace them with beneficial ones, through which the action of the Law of Mind creates anew for me a life that is more worth living.

o o o

Today I will apply this idea to these aspects of my thoughts and actions:

_____

_____

My particular problem, condition, or situation which it can be used to correct is:

_____

_____

YOU HAVE GREAT POSSIBILITIES

There Are Unlimited Resources Within You

Now that you realize that Life holds nothing against you, that It is depriving you of nothing, it would naturally follow that all of It is available to you. What you are is an expression of infinite Intelligence, partaking of Its nature and creativity.

So wherein does your responsibility lie?

Your Unlimited Potential

It would appear that infinite possibilities are available to you. But the stumbling block is that they do not force themselves upon you, rather you have to discover them for yourself and avail yourself of them. Television was always a possibility but it is only just recently that man has availed himself of it. What possibilities reside within man are but little known as yet. What man will be in times to come is difficult to even imagine. But right now, today, you have possibly made but little use of the full capacities you already recognize as being within you, let alone tapped that larger resource which is always available and which you may use only when you come to know that it is there.

You Are Your Greatest Enemy

You have probably been so busy placing limitations on your self-expression and experience in life that you have been unable to enjoy that which you already have, let alone experience a greater degree of livingness.

YOU HAVE GREAT POSSIBILITIES

For the most part you no doubt have denied yourself the very things you want the most. You have let your thoughts dwell on the things you don't want rather than on what you do want, with the result that you have experienced what you have feared the most.

You do have unlimited possibilities in any direction: plus or minus, good or bad, positive or negative. In what way are you using them now—for your benefit or detriment?

The problem that confronts you, if it is a problem, rests in the fact that you need to recognize that there is no limitation to the way you may think, and that there is no question but that your thought is creative in and of your experience in accord with its action through Law.

You Use Only What You Know

The possibility of using the larger potential which is within you depends on the degree to which you become aware of it and consciously use and direct it. This is due to the very nature of Life Itself. Your task is knowing this and using this knowledge.

Who could not desire to experience better health, greater success, more happiness? What person has yet expressed to the fullest the creative artistry within him? Who has completely loved life and all men? The potential ever waits to be used!

Free Yourself

You must learn to stop limiting yourself and start to use to the fullest the abilities and capabilities you already know you have. Then will come the time when you may reach down into the bottomless reservoir of the Infinite within you where lie limitless possibilities which are yours for the recognition and acceptance of them.

The scientist in his discoveries, the artist in his capture of beauty, the poet with his words of depth and meaning, the composer and his immortal melodies, the incurable who is cured, all have reached deeply into the Infinite possibilities. Who has not? To a great extent you have already been doing it unknowingly. Your inspiration, your intuition, your expression of brotherly love, your highest ideals and goals all have their source there.

YOU HAVE GREAT POSSIBILITIES

Infinite Mind has placed no restriction or limitation on your thought. It could not unless It would limit Itself. This the Infinite cannot do. The creativity of your thought is the key to your experience.

You Already Are What You Want To Be

You have to free your thinking from all limitations you have imposed on it, and realize that the limitless potential of good in the universe is accessible to you. Then will you be able to become the greater person you already are but are not fully aware of yet. Then you will be able to experience to a fuller extent, in all aspects of your life, that ideal good which is inherent in Life. You have great possibilities!

MENTAL STIMULANTS

SCIENCE: *We identify the rational element of the human mind with the rational Mind of the Universe, and the creative power of human thought with the creative energy which is the physical world. We take only a small step when we pass from the Energy of modern science to God, the Creator, who said "Let there be light."*
                                                    —Paul E. Sabine

PHILOSOPHY: *The creative force which produces and sustains all that is, reveals itself to me in a way in which I do not get to know it elsewhere ... as something which desires to be creative within me.*
                                                    —Albert Schweitzer

RELIGION: *What is man, that thou art mindful of him? ... Thou madest him to have dominion over the works of thy hands: thou hast put all things under his feet.*
                                                    —Psalm 8:4, 6

YOU HAVE GREAT POSSIBILITIES

THE DIET

There ever lies within me the birthright, the privilege, and the obligation to discover in the depths of my own being the greater person I already am. I no longer limit myself in any respect. From the infinite Source of all things I accept and express greater health. All my creative endeavor, which is but the pressing forth through me of the Divine urge to creativity, is now brought to fuller fruition. Ideas and inspiration flow in an endless stream from the One Mind. Just as every thought in the Mind of God is in its nature creative, so every idea that flows into my mind carries with it the power, the ways and the means of its own accomplishment and fulfillment. In every aspect of my life I expect, I accept, I now experience the continuous dynamic flow of infinite possibility into tangible manifestation. I place no limitations on it. I raise no barriers to it. I let my mind freely roam the entire realm of all possible good, and know that as I think of and claim that good, it is mine.

—Capsule Supplement—

God is not limited, neither is His expression in and through me. I accept and experience in all ways the abundant flow of Life's greater potential.

❁ ❁ ❁

Today I will apply this idea to these aspects of my thoughts and actions:

_____

_____

My particular problem, condition, or situation which it can be used to correct is:

_____

_____

DISCOVERING YOURSELF

You Are in Partnership with the Creator of the Universe

Your consciousness — intelligence and ability to think — is part of infinite Intelligence in you as you. Its thought is creative, and so is yours at the level of your expression of It. You are a cocreator with the One Mind!

As a tangible creation and manifestation of the One Mind, what are you doing about it? What can you do about it? What need you do about it?

There would appear to be a responsibility that is largely unrecognized; an obligation to fulfill that is not fully comprehended. And this comes from not knowing the nature of what you are.

The Value of Discontent

There is a need to discover yourself. To become aware of the Divine urge that is forever pressing forth from the center of you, seeking greater recognition of Itself through you.

You have, time and time again, experienced the creative urge for expression. You must be creative in your life or you feel deeply frustrated, whether your desire for achievement takes the form of a masterpiece of art or a chocolate cake. You must express love, else hate will gnaw within you destroying health and happiness. There must be a givingness in all you do, otherwise you are only depriving yourself.

The universe deprives you of nothing but continually strives to express through you. Any lessening of the discontent you may feel can be achieved only through creative expression. It is this Divine discontent which drives you on toward ever greater accomplishment.

DISCOVERING YOURSELF

Creative Endeavor

All these things you know. You have experienced them. But are you fully aware of their necessity and their larger implications? They are a reflection through you of the very nature of the universe, which is always creative.

You can determine that the patterns of your thought shall be in accord only with the harmonious action of the universe. As you discover that God is not sick, a failure, or unhappy, you will find that there is no reason for you to have these or similar experiences. In fact, when you do have them you are only denying your real identity as a Divine creation.

You Are a Part of Life

Every moment of every day, through the process of what you think, you are establishing the pattern or mold of your experience. What is it going to be? Are you going to let your thinking follow the well-worn paths of race belief in the necessity of sickness, poverty, and unhappiness? Or are you going to stand up and declare to yourself that you know you are a part of Life, claim Its inherent good in and as your experience, and become a cocreator with God at the level of your expression of God?

This you should learn to do. It is a necessity, in fact, if you are to get the most out of living. Whereas previously you may have had the feeling that everything was all wrong with life, now as you discover yourself for what you really are and align the pattern of your thinking with the nature of the Infinite, you will find yourself creative only of good in your life and that of others.

You Are a Cocreator with God

Accept the fact that you are a cocreator with the infinite Creator. You have been all along, but look at some of the things in your life that through ignorance you alone have been responsible for! You can discover and avail yourself of the nature and action of the Infinite at the center of your being, and accept and permit Its fuller expression of good in and through every aspect of your life. When you do you will have discovered yourself.

DISCOVERING YOURSELF

This is the greatest thing any man can do. This is the marvelous adventure in living, the endless achievement of becoming ever more of what you are. There is nothing to limit you, no seeming barriers that cannot be overcome. There is no struggle or battle to wage. The steppingstones to the discovery of the greater *you* are to be found in your increased awareness of the nature of God-Life; your relationship to It and obligation to express It; the removal of any and all limiting concepts or patterns of thought which are preventing Its fuller flow through you. As you discover what you really are, you open the door to a greater experience of all the good that Life has to offer.

MENTAL STIMULANTS

SCIENCE: *The second aspect of God that I recognize is the basis of existence and of life and motivation, which I think of as conscious Power. This Power appears to me as having a special concern for Its conscious creatures who share the responsibility for shaping their part of the world. The opportunity to share with God the shaping of the conditions of life is a tremendous challenge and the great responsibility that comes with freedom.*

—Arthur H. Compton

PHILOSOPHY: *Always there is the creative life of God working in and through us, as we are prepared for it and cooperate with it. We must believe that the forces of the Spirit are stronger than any material forces; "that thoughts rule the world." In our ideal creativeness and the faith which is its inspiration, we are in a small measure architects with God of the universe-builders of the nobler temple of the future.*

—John Elof Boodin

RELIGION: *...as the Father hath life in himself; so hath he given to the Son to have life in himself.*

—John 5:26

DISCOVERING YOURSELF

THE DIET

I know that every man is a creation of God—a Son of God—and I am that Son now. God is forever creating and becoming His creation. The nature of God is never diminished by what He creates, but I have yet to fully awake to all that I am. God is what I am. All of God is where I am. My mind is an individualized expression of the Mind of God. God speaks and it is done. I speak my word and it is creative as my life at the level of my expression and awareness of God. I now declare and affirm that only the perfect, harmonious action of God is what appears in and through my life and experience. I accept the responsibility of causing this to come to pass through the creativeness of my own thought. Today I straighten out my thinking. In full awareness of myself as a cocreator with God, I now declare that from this moment on all the patterns of my thinking shall always be in accord with the greatest possible good, which normally and naturally becomes manifest, through the Law of Mind, in every aspect of my life.

—Capsule Supplement—

I recognize and affirm that the creative action of the spark of Divinity that resides at the center of my being, now unhindered by my negative thinking, goes forth anew into fuller expression in my life.

✿　✿　✿

Today I will apply this idea to these aspects of my thoughts and actions:

_____

_____

My particular problem, condition, or situation which it can be used to correct is:

_____

_____

THE
SECOND
WEEK

The mental diet for the next seven days includes ideas which relate to your attitudes toward your daily life. They will help you to establish a proper frame of mind so that you can more adequately face all the experiences you may encounter, get more joy out of living, and enthusiastically contribute more of the things that are worthwhile for the benefit of yourself and others.

LIVE WITH ENTHUSIASM • HOW TO REMOVE LIMITATIONS

YOU ALWAYS SUCCEED • DEVELOP CONFIDENCE IN YOURSELF

HOW TO CREATE NEW IDEAS • STOP BEING AFRAID

LIFE OWES YOU NOTHING

LIVE WITH ENTHUSIASM

Expression Is the Essence of Life

The salient factor in all living things is a purposeful, constructive action. There is a continual growth and progression toward a goal. This is one of the criteria that scientists use to separate those things which they term alive from the so-called inanimate material of the world.

Are You Alive?

You, of course, are alive; your physical body is powerful evidence of the dynamic purposeful forces of Life active within you. But are you fully alive? Life in Its expression as you has reached the place where you are self-conscious and think. It naturally follows that this activity of Life within you must be purposeful and creative. But the scope of this activity is determined by you. You may be only half alive and not know it!

Why You Must Be Creative

Life, in all of its aspects, is a creative activity. Life in you should be creatively expressed in all ways. The minute the flow of Life is hindered or restricted in one respect there is automatically a reduction of Its flow in other ways. This leads to the inescapable conclusion that if you are not mentally productive you are depriving yourself of a fuller experience of Life physically. A stagnant mind produces a stagnant body, and where there is not a free flow of Life deterioration sets in. The healthy, happy person is the one who is busily engaged in creative and worthwhile endeavors. The size or importance of the endeavor appears to matter little, but the endeavor must have significance for you. You must feel that you are doing something constructive and that there is some purpose in what you are doing.

LIVE WITH ENTHUSIASM

Creative Activities

There are limitless possibilities for creative endeavor. Some people find it in music, painting, or writing. Others discover an outlet for the satisfaction of this Divine urge in gardening, cooking, sewing, and do-it-yourself projects. Very often it is found in normal gainful occupations. Even in what appear to be boring routine tasks there can be discovered an approach to them that permits of a feeling of some kind of creative endeavor. Oddly enough, although compensation may be involved, it seems to have no relationship to the satisfaction derived from being able to express yourself in a purposeful way. Creative you must be. In this respect even the high-salaried corporation president could have less joy in living than the hungry aspiring poet.

Learn To Be Creative

You have a lot to give to yourself and others. As a unique expression of God no one else can contribute what you can. It is up to you to let yourself be all that you can be in your activities. If you are gainfully employed you must in some way regard your work as a constructive, purposeful activity. If you do not you are of mediocre value to your employer and doing yourself a damaging injustice.

If you are bored it is because you are not active. Life is never bored, It is always active. You can decide to be active and express Life any time you want to. A passive existence, just sitting and watching the world go by, needs to be changed. There needs to be an outflow from you to the world about you. There needs to be a giving of what you are.

Your Resources

Re-evaluate yourself. Recognize your resources which ever lie ready to be tapped. Instead of minimizing your present abilities, develop them, for then you open the door for the discovery and use of latent ones which reside at the center of your being.

LIVE WITH ENTHUSIASM

Regardless of how creative you may now be, there is always the continual challenge to use that greater potential that is ever available to you. There is always the more that can be done, that needs to be done, and that you can do providing you do not limit your experience of the flow of creativity from the One Source of all things.

Be Yourself

You must learn to be yourself—an outlet for the activity of Life in you. This is an ever-increasing endeavor for there is no diminishing of this activity except by those limitations you place upon yourself. You were created to be a channel for the expression of Life. Regardless of your position, the nature of your endeavors, or the situation or condition in which you may find yourself, it is an axiom of nature that you must in some way learn to express yourself.

MENTAL STIMULANTS

SCIENCE: *...there is still a higher level in the mental structure of man, a still higher form of energies and activities, realized in varying degrees by different persons—namely, the supraconscious God level of energies and activities. These are frequently designated as "the divine in man." The supraconscious manifests itself in the greatest creative victories of man in the fields of truth, beauty and goodness.*

—Pitirim A. Sorokin

PHILOSOPHY: *Whatever is, is in God, and nothing can exist or be conceived without God.*

—Spinoza

RELIGION: *For it is God which worketh in you both to will and to do of his good pleasure.*

—Philippians 2:13

LIVE WITH ENTHUSIASM

THE DIET

I know that I am a part of Life. Its continual purposeful creativity is evidenced in my mind and body and finds an outlet through what I think and what I do. As I now turn to this infinite Intelligence, recognizing that It is also my intelligence, I permit myself to become an ever-increasing channel for Its creative endeavor. Infinite Mind always fulfills Its every desire. The Divine creative urge within me provides itself with the proper avenues for a complete and full expression and achievement. I am guided and directed into new situations, possess new ideas, discover new ways to be creative in what I am now doing. I become aware of new possibilities within myself enabling me to engage in joyful and happy endeavors. I am supplied with the knowledge, the means, and the ways to become a more active, dynamic channel for the purposefulness of Life. All my creative work is done with ease, sureness, and confidence, for it is not I but infinite Mind that is the doer. As I now express more of what Life is, I more fully experience in all ways the completeness, the wholeness, the perfection, and the harmony that is Its nature.

— Capsule Supplement —

Today in all ways I express more fully the creative activity of Life. I discover more joy and happiness through a greater influx and outflow of Divine ideas.

o   o   o

Today I will apply this idea to these aspects of my thoughts and actions:

_____

_____

My particular problem, condition, or situation which it can be used to correct is:

_____

_____

HOW TO REMOVE LIMITATIONS
Life Does Not Limit You

By definition the universe is limitless, and as such must contain infinite possibilities. Within the bounds of law, physical and spiritual, it appears that there are no restrictions on the purposeful creative activity of man. Everything that has happened, everything that can happen, must of necessity flow from some activity of infinite Intelligence.

Self-limitation

Although you are part of and immersed in That which is infinite, you limit your experience of this terrific potential through self-limitation. As you limit your ideas of what It is, what It can do, you automatically restrict what It can be for you. Life can never become less that It is. But It can never become more to you than you think It is. Your experience in every respect is bounded by what you think It can be for you.

Free Your Thinking

In thinking of any form of abundance in any respect do not think in terms of tangible manifestations of it, but rather of the spiritual cause, the idea, and the Law according to which it becomes manifest. Appearances change, things come and go, but there forever remains the ways and the means for other things to become manifest in your experience. You will always be able to add two and two and get four as an answer. You will always be able to express love and have it returned to you. You will always be able to release a rock from your hand and have it fall to the ground. In everything you are, do, and experience you are fundamentally dealing with basic principles and causes. These never wear out,

HOW TO REMOVE LIMITATIONS

never become exhausted, never refuse to work; but all too often it is felt that they do. When they appear to, the fault lies not in them but in your limited idea as to what they can do for you.

Examine Yourself

A close look at your present position and experience will no doubt reveal that in numerous respects you feel you are limited, that you do not have enough of the good things of life in a universe that is abundant in all ways. It does no good to complain about any lack, that only increases it. The only way you can correct the situation is to do something about it, and the something you must do starts right where you are and with what you are thinking. You are in the position of a man who has an unlimited checking account at the bank but feels his account has only a hundred dollars in it. Whatever situation you may find yourself in, that situation is but a reflection of the amount of good you feel Life can hold for you. You measure your abundance by the pattern of your thinking.

Better Ideas

Fundamental to your experience of more abundance is the development of your concept of what God is. God is the source of, and is, all creation. Don't limit God in whom rest all possibilities. Thought in the Mind of God, or your mind, is the prime creative factor. In your life it is the means by which you measure your share of the limitless. The Law of Mind is always operating according to the pattern of your thinking, making manifest the content of your thought. Also there is the fact that thought itself can know no bounds. So you are confronted with a universe which is limitless, and with thought, the creative factor, which has no limits. If there is not enough abundance in your experience you are using your thought to limit what the universe can be to you, you are refusing to let your thinking expand to include and accept the increased good of which you have need. There is nothing wrong with the universe, or with the principles by which it operates. You have no alibi. The only fault rests in the nature of your thought patterns. You need to have bigger ideas about yourself, your experiences, and the nature of God.

HOW TO REMOVE LIMITATIONS

Expand Your Thinking

Regardless of what it is you feel you should have more of, whether it be wealth, success, health, better relations with others, or more sales, they all resolve themselves back to a thought pattern. A greater experience of anything first requires an awareness that the possibility is available to you, and then a desire and willingness to accept it.

Do Something About It

All of this does not mean that the greater good you desire will suddenly pop into your life. What it does mean is that as you come to know that it can be yours, and as you declare and accept that it is yours and act as though it were yours now, the creativeness of the Law of Mind in action has no choice but to produce it for you. As you unlimit your thinking you open the doors to the influx of That which knows no bounds.

MENTAL STIMULANTS

SCIENCE: *I am apt to regard [prayer]...as all that we yet have for setting into motion that relationship between mind and matter as yet but little understood, but which, in the last analysis, may be more profound than many of us surmise.*

—W. F. G. Swann

PHILOSOPHY: *...that I—I in the widest meaning of the word, that is to say, every conscious mind that has ever said or felt "I"—am the person, if any, who controls the "motions of the atoms" according to the laws of nature.*

—Erwin Schrodinger

RELIGION: *In the beginning was the Word, and the Word was with God, and the Word was God....All things were made by him; and without him was not any thing made that was made.*

—John 1:1, 3

HOW TO REMOVE LIMITATIONS

THE DIET

I know that there is nothing in a limitless universe that bars me from a greater experience of good. I recognize that there is no limit to my good and I place no restrictions on the amount I may accept and use. Wherever there seems to be a lack of any kind, this void is now filled with all that is needed to supply an overflowing abundance. An abundance of all good things fills every phase of my living. In my mental and physical acceptance of it I deprive no one. Although my good may come to me through human channels, it is the creative activity of God that provides it. I recognize myself for what I am, an expression of God, and know that as I turn to Him all that He has is available to me for the accepting. I refuse to let any situation or thought limit my greater experience of good. I am free of all shackles of limitation and partake of the abundance of the universe which can and does fill my every need. I open my mind, encompass the greatest good I can possibly conceive, and without a question of doubt accept and act as if it were mine now—God does the rest.

— Capsule Supplement —

Today I live the abundant life. Mentally and emotionally I know that the action of infinite Intelligence now creates in my experience those things which correspond to my conviction that my every good need is fulfilled.

o o o

Today I will apply this idea to these aspects of my thoughts and actions:

_____

_____

My particular problem, condition, or situation which it can be used to correct is:

_____

_____

YOU ALWAYS SUCCEED

It Is Impossible for You To Fail

Strange as it sounds, it is impossible for you to fail. For if you fail you have succeeded in being a failure!

What Is Success?

For the most part people feel that they are a success in an endeavor when it has a favorable outcome, and a failure when it is not accomplished. But this is not necessarily true. Closer consideration will show that success is the achievement of the dominant idea you have in mind, and what you achieve always corresponds to your thinking. In this respect you never fail, you always succeed. Whether the outcome of your endeavor is favorable or unfavorable does not enter into the matter.

At What Are You Succeeding?

You are accomplishing something all the time. Whether or not you like the result is for you to determine. If your experiences are unfavorable perhaps it is time to start to succeed in something different, something more to your liking. For the most part people seem to spend their time and effort in achieving those things which they don't want. How are you doing in this respect? In what ways are you succeeding? How is your health? How do you get along with other people? How is business? All good? all bad? or a little of both? You can start right now to have a more enjoyable experience of success, but it can only begin with the way you are thinking.

YOU ALWAYS SUCCEED

The Start of Success

Inasmuch as you always succeed in experiencing the content of your thought, it becomes a matter of vital concern as to what you are thinking. It is a matter of elementary logic that you cannot experience health if all your thoughts are of ill-health. That you cannot have friends if you dislike people. That you cannot have a profitable business if you consistently know it is going to fail. Of course there are many variations in the way you can think. For instance, you can spend all your time thinking about ill-health, or divide it up so that half the time you think about ill-health and the other half about health, or you can get completely over to the plus side and think only about health. The outcome of these various patterns of thinking is quite obvious. There only remains for you to decide in what way you want to succeed—what you want to have become your experience.

Success Is Automatic

There is nothing you can do about the fact that your pattern of thinking is successfully, fully, and completely manifested in your experience. Your thought is the pattern, the form, the channel for the creative action of the Law of Mind to produce tangible situations, conditions, and experiences that correspond to your thought. They are obviously good when your thoughts are good, but when they are not it is a difficult situation to face. But face it you must. Your only solution is to make certain that you keep your thinking under control. Entertain only those ideas which have a good content, which are free from worry, fear, and anxiety. Expect the favorable, not the unfavorable, to happen to you. The process of thought-becoming-thing is automatic; your responsibility rests in controlling the nature of your thoughts.

Success Insurance

One of the toughest things you will ever have to do is to stand guardian over what you establish as your consistent patterns of thinking. Yet it is the most important thing you can ever do. You alone have the responsibility of determining what you are going to think, and in this responsibility rests the nature of your success, whether it will be good or bad.

YOU ALWAYS SUCCEED

You need to decide right now that all your experiences are going to be favorable, that life is going to be a joyous adventure. Eliminate all ideas contrary to such concepts, do not permit yourself to accept the necessity of negative conditions and situations about you. Your experience of a happy life is insured to the extent you maintain favorable ideas in your thought. But this is not a part-time undertaking, neither is it a Pollyanna attitude. Rather, it of necessity must be a dynamic and positive mental act built on a conviction, beyond all doubt, that such ideas are creative of your experience. Not that they are creative of themselves, but that they are the channel through which the creative action of infinite Intelligence flows.

Start All Over Again

Regardless of what unfavorable ways you may have succeeded in in the past, they have no hold on you once you decide to start to succeed in a favorable way. Every thought is the start of a new sequence of events and you can have them be to your liking. Each moment is a new beginning, so start now to succeed in the things that make life a joyful, happy experience.

MENTAL STIMULANTS

SCIENCE: *Just as tragedy and comedy can be written using the same letters so many varied events in this world can be realized by the same atoms as long as they take up different positions and describe different movements.*

—Democritus

PHILOSOPHY: *The recognition of God...with the cosmic drive of which the life-personality is the spearhead is the only road to self-fulfillment.*

—Louis Berman

RELIGION: *So shall my word be that goeth forth out of my mouth: it shall not return unto me void, but it shall accomplish that which I please, and it shall prosper in the thing whereto I sent it.*

—Isaiah 55:11

YOU ALWAYS SUCCEED

THE DIET

Today, from this moment on, I determine to succeed only in those things which are worthy, beneficial, and provide the greatest good. I let go of all ideas and concepts which are contrary to the good life I desire to live. Whether it be in relation to my health, those about me, or my affairs, I establish now in my mind ideas embodying the way I desire things to be. I consistently maintain these ideas and let nothing sway my conviction that they represent my experience as it is to become. I am rightly guided in establishing and maintaining those patterns of thought that correspond to the nature of God, which is good. I refuse to let myself be influenced by negative conditions and situations. I know that the creative action of the Law of Mind manifests in tangible form the content of my thought. Therefore I let my thought dwell only on things of benefit to myself and others, and I now expect only good things to happen to me. As I establish in my mind a pattern of thinking that accepts only good as my experience, this is what comes into being. I now succeed only in those things which are good.

— Capsule Supplement —

Success is always mine, and I now determine and declare that my thoughts—the pattern of my success—shall be like the thoughts of God which are only good.

✿   ✿   ✿

Today I will apply this idea to these aspects of my thoughts and actions:

_____

_____

My particular problem, condition, or situation which it can be used to correct is:

_____

_____

DEVELOP CONFIDENCE IN YOURSELF

Learn To Do the Right Things in the Right Way

Naturally you like to feel that you are doing the right thing at the right time. But too often in looking back you realize that you should have acted other than the way you did. To all intents and purposes you were sure that you did your best at the time. But did you? Did you use all the resources at your command?

You Are Not Alone

When you arrive at any decision regarding a course of action you carefully evaluate all the information available, judge the possible outcome of various decisions, and then select what appears to be the most favorable. In spite of how much you might know, how much advice you might be able to secure, still the most desirous results may not be achieved. It is at this point that is it necessary to remember that you are not alone! You are a part of Life, an expression of infinite Intelligence, and have access to the One Mind in which all things are known.

Your Partnership with Life

You may be the one who feels that you can stand on your own two feet, achieve all that you desire to achieve by yourself; that you are entirely self-sufficient. How wrong can you be! Let us see just how independent you can be. Who raised you as a baby? Who makes your clothes from fiber to fabric to finished product? How do you get your food from seed to the vegetable in the dish? But to get a little more personal, how did you heal that cut on your finger? By what process did you convert the steak you ate last night into energy for today's endeavors? If you ever really tried to be independent and isolate yourself from

DEVELOP CONFIDENCE IN YOURSELF

these activities you would find yourself in a sorry predicament. You gratefully accept and take for granted your dependency on all of these functions of living. But when it comes to thinking, do you feel that it is your own personal achievement?

Are You Only Half-thinking

You have discovered that *that* within you which thinks is not something isolated from the rest of Life, but instead is an activity and expression of Life within you. As you come to realize that your mind is not your mind but an aspect of infinite Mind, you will find that all too often you have tried to go your own way without recognizing the greater potential that is always available to you. In every situation, in every decision and every action, you should accept and permit the influx and guidance of that Mind greater than your mind. Don't confine your thinking to what you think you know when an unlimited reservoir of knowledge is available to you. Why accept the lesser when the greater is always yours for the accepting?

The Course of Action

There is no one living who of himself can possibly know, without any question of doubt, the perfect decision or course of action. One may make it appear that he does, but such a thing is impossible to man's worldly wisdom. It is only when all that is known is related to the Mind which knows all things that it can be said right action results. When you need to make a decision, when you need to determine a course of action, there must be a gathering together of all the facts, all the evidence, all the information relative to the situation. This done, you must then consciously subject them to the action of infinite Mind. And in so doing you must have a firm faith and conviction that you will be guided and directed in a manner that will result in the greatest possible good for all concerned. History is filled with dramatic illustrations of Divine guidance, and the thing for you to remember is that this is not a sometime thing nor just for special people; it is always available to those who avail themselves of it.

DEVELOP CONFIDENCE IN YOURSELF

A Good Habit

All of this does not mean that you stop thinking, that you just sit and wait for bright ideas to come to you, or that you remain in a state of indecision. Rather, you need to use your ability to think to the utmost degree and at the same time to *know* that the Power that thinks as you rightly directs and guides you. The course of events which follows this type of thinking may often conform to what you first felt should occur, and then again you may find yourself proceeding in an entirely different direction, one *you* had not originally thought of but which leads to more favorable results than you ever anticipated.

Acknowledge Your Partnership

Your life can be so much more worthwhile if you acknowledge your partnership with Life and continuously accept Its activity in all that you do. The ability to make right decisions, to have right action occur in your experiences, rests entirely on your knowing that infinite Intelligence is active in and through your thinking and actions, and that in everything connected with your life you are rightly, Divinely guided.

MENTAL STIMULANTS

SCIENCE: *Human thought is an integral part of the universe, of the cosmos....*

—Lecomte DuNouy

PHILOSOPHY: *...we inhabit an invisible spiritual environment from which our help comes, our soul being mysteriously one with a larger one whose instruments we are.*

—Henry James

RELIGION: *I can of mine own self do nothing...the Father that dwelleth in me, he doeth the works.*

—John 5:30; 14:10

DEVELOP CONFIDENCE IN YOURSELF

THE DIET

I have confidence in my ability to achieve every good thing I undertake, for I know that from the Divine Center within I am properly guided and directed to do the right thing at the right time in the right way. As I am a focal point of infinite Intelligence, in which all things are known, there is made known to me that which I should do for the greatest good for myself and those about me. I cease hesitating, wondering, and doubting, and release to the action of Divine Mind the making of those correct decisions which guide me into a greater experience of joyous living. In God there is only right action, and as I now turn to and accept His action in my life today, all is as it should be. God's Life is my life, God's Intelligence is my intelligence, and I now remove all ideas of separation from, and gratefully acknowledge my unity with, that Power greater than I am. As I now let God become a partner in all that I do there follows increased confidence in living.

— Capsule Supplement —

Today, through the action of infinite Intelligence at the center of my being, I am rightly guided in all my decisions and actions so that the greatest good comes to me and to others.

❊　❊　❊

Today I will apply this idea to these aspects of my thoughts and actions:

_____

_____

My particular problem, condition, or situation which it can be used to correct is:

_____

_____

HOW TO CREATE NEW IDEAS

There Is a Limitless Source of Inspiration

Everyone has had the experience at one time or another of having an unusually bright idea. Some have them more often than others; some seem to be continually inspired. Such moments of insight are called hunches, bright ideas, inspirations, intuitions, strokes of genius, and other similar terms. But they all add up to the same thing—something new has come into the mind.

Spontaneous Ideas

The entire history of man has been highlighted by the sudden appearance of ideas which seem to have sprung from nowhere. In some cases there appears to have been a slight foundation or background for the new idea and at other times it has been completely unique. No doubt this has been your own experience also. Without any rhyme or reason you suddenly find yourself in possession of an idea frought with possibilities, an idea about something to which in all probability you had never given any particular consideration. Or you discover in an instant a solution to a difficult problem, a solution which is as astounding as it is simple. Where do such ideas come from? and is it possible to find more of them?

Where Do New Ideas Come From?

Many people who are creative most of their lives find that there come times when something literally seems to possess them and they are driven into a period of continuous creative endeavor which will not let them go. Lack of sleep or food seems not to matter, the work must go on until completed, or they collapse from exhaustion. Such people appear to have tapped a source of creativity which insists on being expressed.

HOW TO CREATE NEW IDEAS

Others have but a momentary contact with this source, or just a sudden flash. But that such a source is there, and available all the time, must be a fact or else no one at any time could possibly have such experiences.

You Can Have New Ideas

If you will recall Emerson's statement that "There is one mind common to all individual men," you can see how you can have access to that infinite Source of ideas. Your mind is an aspect or individualization of the One Mind, and as such can avail itself of Its creative energy. You may not become a genius and have your mind be a continuous fountainhead of new and brilliant ideas, but there is no question about the fact that you can have more new and constructive ideas than you are now experiencing.

It's Fun to Be Inspired

Like everyone else, you get a big thrill out of a new idea. It stimulates your mind to greater activity, it acts like a tonic to your body, and you have a happier, more joyous outlook on life in general. Although you may not be able to tap this Source continually, there is every indication that you can develop an attitude and cultivate a way of thinking that will enable you more frequently to avail yourself of Its resources. In fact, properly approached, the process of acquiring new ideas, of discovering new inspirations, can become a sort of game in which you will continually become more proficient.

How to Start

In your search for new ideas, after you have brought to bear on the situation all the knowledge you have, you need to remember that your mind is not *your* mind, but an individualization of infinite Intelligence. In this knowledge you can reach a point where you surrender the thought that you are the prime source of your every idea and become a more perfect instrument for Its action. Nothing about this is new, rather it is attested to by the outstanding accomplishments of many of the greatest men and women of the arts and sci-

HOW TO CREATE NEW IDEAS

ences, or business and human relations. They all have recognized only one Source to which to turn, and you may turn there too.

Expect New Ideas

One of the best things you can do for the cultivation of new ideas is to *expect* that you will have them. You need not be specific about the influx of inspiration, or determine beforehand what the nature of it should be. There should be the cultivation of an expectant attitude, a conscious effort to keep your mind open to such an influx. Start the day with the conviction that many wonderful new ideas are going to come to you, that you are going to encounter new situations which will provide you with unusual opportunities. If you can develop the habit of maintaining an open mind you will soon find that your life and experience can take on a whole new meaning. Your consciousness is what you really are, so let it manifest more of what it actually is. Don't keep your mind in chains but let it be free to soar to discover more of the wonder of itself.

MENTAL STIMULANTS

SCIENCE: *Consciousness has other functions besides those of a rather inefficient measuring machine; and knowledge may attain to other truths besides those which correlate sensory impressions.*

— Arthur Eddington

PHILOSOPHY: *...if we are to make scientific progress, we must trust our minds to reach out beyond the visible by an act of faith in ourselves, in the world, in the creative Force which is acting.*

— Ralph Tyler Flewelling

RELIGION: *Be still, and know that I am God....*

— Psalm 46:10

HOW TO CREATE NEW IDEAS

THE DIET

This day, like every day, is a new beginning. It is filled with a wonderful potential of new ideas and new inspiration. Regardless of the situation in which I may be, I know there is always available to me the limitless resources of the One Mind, of which my mind is a part. I discard all thoughts about any possible lack, and open my mind to the influx of ideas that are new, wonderful, and filled with inspiration. The activity of infinite Intelligence floods my consciousness, providing me with creative, worthwhile ideas that can bring good to myself and my fellow man. I never know a dearth of ideas or inspiration for I now recognize there is but One Source from which they come and I accept It as always active in me. I am ever alert to ideas seeking to find an outlet through me. I recognize them and act upon them, knowing that they come provided with the ways and means for their fulfillment. God created me as an expression of Himself and as a channel through which He may continually express. I look within my own consciousness, opening the doors for the inflow of Divine Wisdom. A new life of new ideas now is mine.

— Capsule Supplement —

I know my mind is of the One Mind and is an ever-increasing channel for the flow of inspiration and creative ideas which open up a whole new world of richer living for myself and others.

∘   ∘   ∘

Today I will apply this idea to these aspects of my thoughts and actions:

_____

_____

My particular problem, condition, or situation which it can be used to correct is:

_____

_____

STOP BEING AFRAID

Don't Defeat Yourself

For the most part people seem to go through life being afraid of one thing or another. In fact, many appear to go out of their way to find things to be apprehensive about. Their thoughts emphasize what they are fearful of and overlook those things in which they may have complete confidence and security. In spite of all appearances and situations, of one thing you may be sure, and that is that there is nothing in the nature of Life Itself that holds anything against you.

Limit Yourself

If there is ever a need to impose limitations upon yourself it is in connection with the amount of trouble you borrow. In this respect you should make sure that your credit is no good. Like most people, you probably are not content with the problems of the immediate moment but develop a fearsome attitude about what you will encounter tomorrow, the day after, next month, and next year; you have completely forgotten the childlike trust you used to have in your world. Instead of maintaining a calm assurance that things will be all right, you apparently have developed a perverse nature which looks out on the world with a jaundiced eye and the only things you see or anticipate are not good. This attitude of course takes all the joy and happiness out of living. Even when you should be enjoying life you find yourself immersed in a maelstrom of fear about what might happen.

There is a need to re-educate yourself with the knowledge that neither infinite Intelligence nor Its expression as your world of experience can possibly be against Itself. What you do find in your experience about which you might be fearful would appear to be nothing but the reflection of your own negative attitudes. As Job said: "... the thing which I greatly feared is come upon me."

STOP BEING AFRAID

Welcome Change

A great many people resent any change in or from their present situation. They fight it and are fearful of it. Actually, change should be welcome for it is only through change that better things may come to pass. When change is feared it is because there is a lack of recognition that the very basis of all existence rests on the fact that there is continual change. If change did not occur there would be complete stagnation of all living things. So it is with your own life and experience; if everything is at a complete standstill, regardless at what level it may be, stagnation sets in and this means that only deterioration can result. Changes should be welcomed, welcomed with the knowledge that they can be for the better, and there should be an elimination of the fear that any change means catastrophe.

Re-educate Yourself

No doubt you, the same as most people, have carefully educated yourself in the ability to search out countless things in every situation about which to be fearful. Just as you have carefully developed this negative ability, you can re-educate yourself to look for the favorable things which you may encounter. In spite of a tendency to always have a morbid approach to life, you can reverse this pattern of thinking and develop a more cheerful outlook. The wisdom in doing this rests in the fact that you always seem to find what you are looking for.

You Make Your Own Life

As much as you would like to avoid the responsibility of what you experience in daily living, it is largely the result of your own thinking. If your thinking is constantly dwelling on all the negative things which could possibly be encountered, you will find yourself buried in trouble. Not because there is anything in God or nature that desires you to be miserable, but rather because it is such things that you are intent on finding. You literally create and discover your difficulties. The only things that can really bedevil you are your own apprehensions.

STOP BEING AFRAID

Confident Living

You need to develop confidence in the fact that life can be joyous and happy. Living is not an eternal battle against an adverse nature and there is no necessity for you to be continually immersed in a fog of anxiety. There is no need for life to be a fearful experience, regardless of what area of your experience you may now be concerned about.

Anticipate the Best

Confident living can begin and fearful living cease when you realize that life is a process of continual change which can always be a change for the better. You alone choose what life shall be to you, so choose carefully. Learn to think about and accept for yourself only the best that it has to offer. This does not mean that you should develop a wishful-thinking attitude, but rather implies that you should develop a constructive and dynamic pattern of thinking that is productive of the good things life can offer.

MENTAL STIMULANTS

SCIENCE: *...we do not walk upon an alien earth and...something in the universe corresponds to human intelligence.*

—N. J. Berrill

PHILOSOPHY: *The image of God is found essentially and personally in all mankind. Each possesses it whole, entire and undivided....we are the image of God...the source in us of all our life....*

—Jan van Ruysbroeck

RELIGION: *...I will fear no evil: for thou art with me; thy rod and thy staff they comfort me.*

—Psalm 23:4

STOP BEING AFRAID

THE DIET

I acknowledge and accept that my life fundamentally is good and that all that appears otherwise does not belong to it. There is nothing I need fear for the Life that flows through me can desire only the best of all possible things for Itself. I now accept the responsibility of choosing that which I shall experience. I discard fear of whatever nature, and as I release my fears they cease being creative of adverse experiences. I am no longer afraid, but live in complete confidence that the Power that made me and sustains me now makes clear and smooth my way. I eliminate those patterns of thinking which attract to me that which I do not want, and focus my attention on the good things I desire. I start living in faith, a faith that is productive of a richer, more joyous life. I live with a sense of security that the right thing is always done in the right way at the right time for my greater expression and experience of the Spirit of Life that resides at the center of my being. My faith is no longer placed in what I do not desire, but only in the good of which I wish to partake. I permit God's Creativeness to flow through me to establish a new life of happiness. All possible good flows from God and is mine to accept, and I do accept it now.

— Capsule Supplement —

I now declare that my faith is soundly based in the good I desire. Fear of any kind is removed and replaced with a complete confidence that God is only good and that this good now fills my every experience.

❈   ❈   ❈

Today I will apply this idea to these aspects of my thoughts and actions:

_____

_____

My particular problem, condition, or situation which it can be used to correct is:

_____

_____

LIFE OWES YOU NOTHING

Living Is What You Make It

The cause of a great many of the troubles people encounter rests in the fact that they seem to have developed a sort of lethargy, which demands that everything be brought to them on a silver platter without their having to do anything about it. This is a nice idea if it would work, but it doesn't, for it overlooks the fact that basic and fundamental to all existence is activity and creativity. If this dictum is ignored living is deprived of all meaning.

The World Does Not Owe You a Living

Do you feel that the world owes you a living, that life should provide you with all your desires and needs without your doing anything about it? The truth of the matter is that all you could possibly need has already been provided for you! There is no reason for any person to sit back and complain that the world has done him wrong, has withheld the things that make living worthwhile. As long as you acknowledge that the Mind back of the universe is intelligent and within It rests the possibility of all good things, then you can realize that everything has already been given you, is ever accessible to you. The problem is to what degree and extent you are able to recognize and accept this.

Your Great Debt

Life owes you nothing but you are eternally in debt to Life. You are the one who is withholding yourself from Life. What do you owe, and to whom do you owe it? You are only able to receive to the extent to which you are able to give. To start with, you are alive,

LIFE OWES YOU NOTHING

an expression of the One Life. To the extent you are able to embody and express what you feel must be Its fundamental nature, to that extent you are able to experience more of It. Life has been given to you, now it is up to you to do something with it. Life is good, creative, dynamic, purposeful, and joyous, and you have to express these qualities. You have to let them flow through you into the world about you. If you have the idea that life has done you wrong, the only thing that really has happened is that you have done yourself wrong.

Continuous Conflict

If you feel that life is a continual conflict, you unintentionally are isolating yourself from the Source which can fulfill your every need. The battle you must wage is not with the world, the argument you must win is not with God, but with yourself. In many respects you are your own worst enemy. When your thoughts and acts are constructive, then you will find that you already have what you once thought was owed to you. Then all conflict and struggle is dissolved.

A Down Payment

You can make a down payment on your debt and start to eliminate a feeling that Life owes you something by this simple procedure: stop feeling sorry for yourself and begin to use your God-given ability to think in a constructive manner. Start to live now, for Life can never be more to you than It is right now. It can never provide you with more than you can consciously accept. When you change your pattern of thinking, and concern yourself with what you can contribute to Life, you will be surprised at what you will start receiving.

Giving versus Gimme

Certain sayings have become so familiar that the truths they contain are overlooked. Such ideas as "The gift is most to the giver"; "Give, and it shall be given unto you"; "And as ye would that men should do to you, do ye also to them likewise," should be re-examined. The world can supply you with abundant living, but not on the basis that it is owed to you. You must become an active participant in life, contributing the most that you have in the best manner possible.

LIFE OWES YOU NOTHING

Definite Action

You are not dealing with pretty platitudes, nice ideas, or beautiful sayings. Instead you realize that you are living in a lawful universe and that, regardless of the experience about which you may be concerned, things happen only as a result of an adequate cause. You cannot receive without first giving, and what you receive is in direct proportion to the extent of the giving of your thought, time, and abilities. Proper creative thought, backed up with appropriate action, opens the doorway for the universe to reciprocate with abundance, "good measure, pressed down ... and running over."

MENTAL STIMULANTS

SCIENCE: *... mental and spiritual forces ... do have operative effect, and are indeed of decisive importance in the highly practical business of working out human destiny, and they are not supernatural, not outside man but within him.*

—Julian Huxley

PHILOSOPHY: *God created man in His own image and likeness, i.e., made him a creator too, calling him to free spontaneous activity and not to formal obedience to His power. Free creativeness is the creature's answer to the great call of its Creator.*

—Nicolai Berdyaev

RELIGION: *And I say unto you, Ask, and it shall be given you; seek, and ye shall find; knock, and it shall be opened unto you.*

—Luke 11:9

LIFE OWES YOU NOTHING

THE DIET

All that is good, fine, and wonderful in my world is mine to have and enjoy. Life withholds nothing from me, Life owes me nothing. In this knowledge and awareness I redirect and repattern my thinking so that I discover new abilities within myself, and I am guided into new ways and means of expressing them. The more I awake to the inner urge of Life to creatively express Itself through what I am, the more I am surrounded with all that contributes to a richer experience of living. My thoughts and acts are causative factors to which the Universe must respond with corresponding effects. I am responsible for my experience and I now affirm that infinite Mind, acting in and as my mind, directs, guides, and stimulates my thought so that it becomes creative in the best possible manner for the establishing in my life of the greatest possible good. I no longer wait for God to give me that which I may need, for I know that all that there is has already been given. I now consciously acknowledge the gift and accept it as mine. My thought and action express my belief and as I give of myself to life I am abundantly rewarded.

— Capsule Supplement —

Life becomes to me what I am to It. Today my every thought and act is my givingness to the world of my highest concept of what I believe God is, and the lawful creative activity of God returns to me in tangible form the good I have affirmed is mine.

° ° °

Today I will apply this idea to these aspects of my thoughts and actions:

_____

_____

My particular problem, condition, or situation which it can be used to correct is:

_____

_____

THE THIRD WEEK

The following seven days of the diet offer ideas which are of vital importance in connection with your affairs and relationships. They apply to your every undertaking and association, and can be used for business or any activity which is an endeavor on your part to be creative, productive, and of service to others. They are vital aids to fuller, richer living and achievement.

THE ART OF GETTING ALONG WITH PEOPLE

MAKE YOUR AFFAIRS PROSPER • HOW TO BUILD SECURITY

LEARN TO LIKE YOURSELF • DISCOVER YOUR PLACE IN LIFE

PEACE OF MIND CAN BE YOURS • USING THE POWER OF LOVE

THE ART OF
GETTING ALONG WITH PEOPLE

People Do Not Need To Be Problems

Harmonious living largely depends upon the nature of your relationships with others; in your home, place of work, or casual encounters. You are influenced by and dependent upon others, by what they mean to you and what you mean to them. You cannot avoid contacting people so it becomes a matter of great importance that your contacts are of a harmonious nature. Whether your contacts with others present problems rests not in others, but in yourself.

Know Yourself

One of the first steps involved in being able to get along with other people is to learn to get along with yourself. This may sound strange but upon careful analysis you may find that you are having a running battle with yourself in one way or another. Before you can get along with others your own house must be in order. Properly understood, this means that you should get rid of all your jealousies, hatreds, resentments, and dislikes of others. Life has nothing against any other expression of Itself. If you can bring yourself to a realization of this, then you will find that you have a new foundation on which to start creating happier relationships.

Life Is a Mirror

People can be to you only what you are to them. Not only in the way you act, but in the way you think they reflect back to you what you really are. Regardless of the way you may act toward others, it is what you actually think about them that determines their reactions to you. You cannot have a smile on your face and hatred in your thoughts and have harmony prevail. Thought is too powerful and creative a thing for you to believe you

THE ART OF GETTING ALONG WITH PEOPLE

could get by with presenting a false front to the world. You first have to become what you would have another person be to you. To have a friend, you must first be a friend. You come right back to the basic proposition of cause and effect.

Molehills Out of Mountains

Very often some minor incident may cause you to become irritated with another person. After this you studiously look for other things about that person that can irritate you. The more you search for them the more you will create them out of the process of your own thought. The whole process keeps growing like a rolling snowball until it is entirely out of control and a real serious problem results which causes nothing but damage and harm. Do not attempt to place any blame on the other person; you need but deal with yourself. Start by dismissing every negative thought you have about the other person, and in some way or other discover something about him that you can like. As soon as you have found one such trait you will discover others. In this manner you can build up a mental concept of the other person that is likeable to you. As you maintain this mental image of him, this is what creates and establishes a harmonious relationship and makes a bad one evaporate.

You Can't Divide Yourself

Do not forget the fact that you cannot divide yourself into pieces. Whatever you may feel toward some people will be reflected in the way you feel toward all people. You cannot hate and love at the same time. As much as you may think you are succeeding, each pattern of thought will color all the others. For this reason, to the extent you permit yourself to have inharmonious relationships in certain areas of experience, you will be depriving yourself of a large degree of harmony in others.

Eliminate Faults

You are as much a part of Life as the next person, and in Life there is no place for jealousy, hatred, ill will, and other negative emotions. All you need be concerned with is

THE ART OF GETTING ALONG WITH PEOPLE

to express yourself at all times in the best possible manner, to the best of your ability, and in conformance with your highest concepts. Once you start to do this, in spite of what your present relationships may be, you will discover that as you eliminate your own faults you will at the same time be removing what you have considered faulty reactions of others toward you.

Like Begets Like

It is an inevitable and immutable fact that like begets like. Your relationships with others rest entirely upon the pattern of your own thinking. The actions and attitudes toward you by the members of your family, your business associates, your neighbors and casual acquaintances are but reflections of how you feel toward them. In order to get along with people it is necessary first to establish concepts of harmonious relationships in your own mind and act accordingly.

MENTAL STIMULANTS

SCIENCE: *Love is the demonstratively active involvement in the welfare of another in such a manner that one not only contributes to the survival of the other, but does so in a creatively enlarging manner.*

— Ashley Montagu

PHILOSOPHY: *...it is only the finite that has wrought and suffered; the infinite lies stretched in smiling repose.*

— Ralph Waldo Emerson

RELIGION: *Therefore all things whatsoever ye would that men should do to you, do ye even so to them: for this is the law and the prophets.*

— Matthew 7:12

THE ART OF GETTING ALONG WITH PEOPLE

THE DIET

Today I firmly establish in my mind that I am at peace with myself and have harmonious relationships with all those about me. I no longer inhibit the flow through me of the love which God has for all His creation. I rid my mind of all negative attitudes toward others and express only love, consideration, and appreciation for them. As I let my thought dwell solely on the desirable qualities in others and overlook the rest, that which I overlook ceases to exist for me. I first discover in myself all those qualities which I would find in others. Then, regardless of present relationships, I know and declare that they can be to me only what I believe them to be. As I cooperate with them, offering the best and finest that I have, there is a similar response which establishes a cooperative effort for the fuller enjoyment of a happier, more harmonious life for all. As I now make a greater effort to reflect the real nature of Life in my thoughts and acts, all my relationships with others develop into a mutual endeavor to express and experience the abundant good that Life affords.

— Capsule Supplement —

Today and every day there is established between myself and everyone with whom I associate a harmonious relationship which is a reflection of the love and good will I bear toward them. All differences of the past are removed and replaced with an increasing mutual understanding and endeavor.

❀　❀　❀

Today I will apply this idea to these aspects of my thoughts and actions:

_____

_____

My particular problem, condition, or situation which it can be used to correct is:

_____

_____

MAKE YOUR AFFAIRS PROSPER

You Live in the Midst of Abundance

Why should you be prosperous? Fundamentally, Life is never stingy, never lacking; there is a superabundance of all that is. Nature is prolific in every respect. One look about you and you can see this for yourself. Have you reason to suppose that Life's abundance stops where you begin?

What Does Prosperity Mean?

It would seem reasonable to assume that prosperity means more than the bare necessities for existence. This would apply to your own life, to your business endeavors, to your every good undertaking. Life is productive and creative and should continue to be so in your experience in whatever respect you desire. You should have whatever is necessary to provide a joyous and happy life. But this means that those good things you desire to come to you must in no way deprive another of what may belong to him. Out of the limitless productivity of the universe enough can be provided for the prosperity of all without limiting or depriving anyone.

How Does Prosperity Start?

Quite a few years ago it was a common expression that prosperity was just around the corner. It was a wonderful sentiment, but far from practical. There remained the problem of what corner and when it would be rounded. The one type of thinking that needs to be avoided is that prosperity is just around a corner, that it will come tomorrow, or the next day. If this kind of thinking is maintained you soon discover that the prosperity you desire is a future thing and will always remain so as long as you so consider it. What you are interested in is prosperity *now*.

MAKE YOUR AFFAIRS PROSPER

First Steps

If your experience is determined and established by the pattern of your thinking, the obvious conclusion is that you have to start to create a frame of mind, a process of thinking, that embodies prosperity as your present state of affairs. Any good undertaking can be a thriving, abundant endeavor, but only when you acknowledge that it is happening *now*, not in the future. This is not a process of blinding yourself to present circumstances or situations but a down-to-earth, practical application of cause and effect.

Prosperity More than a State of Mind

The prosperous person knows that he is prosperous and that he always will be. There is an inner conviction that permits of no doubts. When you reach such a state of belief it is then that the creative activity of infinite Mind takes over and creates in your experience a tangible reproduction of the pattern of your thinking. There is no limit to the creative action of Life, but there rests in your thought the ability to determine how it will be creative for you. The fact that you may not be more prosperous than you now are is the result of the limitations you place on what Life can do for you.

Redirect Your Thinking

For the most part the attainment of prosperity rests upon your ability to stop deploring what little you have—thinking only about the voids in your experience. There needs to be established a definite and specific concept, a mental equivalent, of those things that you desire to possess. Think, believe, and act as though you have them right now. Be thankful for whatever good you already possess, knowing that to it is added whatever manner of prosperity is needed for more worthwhile living. Once you can redirect your thinking in this manner and keep it clear, concise, and specific, there is nothing that possibly can prevent it from becoming a tangible part of your experience.

MAKE YOUR AFFAIRS PROSPER

Accept Prosperity

It has been said that God loves a prosperous man, and probably rightly so, for God prospers in all He does. To the degree that you are not prosperous you are denying the creative activity of God in you as you. Living should not be a thing of limitation or deprivation. The acceptance of abundance starts with the building up in your mind of a conviction that God does not favor others and ignore you. There is some truth in the saying that God helps those who help themselves. To what extent have you been helping yourself to, or depriving yourself of, the abundance of the universe?

New Experiences

New experiences of living are ever open to you when you reach the point where you can firmly and consistently maintain in your pattern of thinking that the abundance you desire, the prosperity you wish to enjoy, is yours *now*. This constant belief, coupled with emotions and actions that reflect it, is a causative factor that will not and cannot be denied by God's creative action as Law, which responds by corresponding, making manifest in any aspect of your experience the prosperity pattern of thinking you have established.

MENTAL STIMULANTS

SCIENCE: *If ... Spirit is limitless creative power, it can provide an inexhaustible reservoir of help and strength from which man can draw freely at his will.*

— Edmund W. Sinnott

PHILOSOPHY: *All forces are potentially present in man and the universe continues the creative process through him.*

— Sarvepalli Radhakrishnan

RELIGION: *... What things soever ye desire, when ye pray, believe that ye receive them, and ye shall have them.*

— Mark 11:24

MAKE YOUR AFFAIRS PROSPER

THE DIET

There is no limit to the abundance, the prolific creativity that resides in the universe. I know that I am part of and not separate from the infinite Intelligence in which all things reside and have their being. In this knowledge and conviction I know that God's creative action continues to manifest itself through the pattern of thinking that I maintain. There is no limit to God and whatever may appear as a need in my experience is abundantly filled as I know and believe that it is filled. Whatever good I undertake, whatever beneficial goals I desire to accomplish, whatever I feel is necessary for a fuller, richer enjoyment of living is successfully fulfilled. All that I wish to do and accomplish that is consistent with good, and neither deprives nor harms anyone, is mine to attain as I now believe that it is mine. The more prosperous I am, the more enjoyment I get out of living, the more I am able to help others, the more I am expressing the God-Life that flows through me. I let go of all ideas of limitation and accept the abundance and prosperity that is the very nature of God's being and creation. In everything I do I am prosperous; I am immersed in an abundance of all good things. A new doorway now opens for me and I enjoy a richer experience of living.

— Capsule Supplement —

The universe is a limitless, abundant, prosperous creation and activity of God. I now accept His Life as my life and all that He possesses now becomes available to me to have and experience. I let loose of limitation and accept prosperity in all things.

❋ ❋ ❋

Today I will apply this idea to these aspects of my thoughts and actions:

_____

_____

My particular problem, condition, or situation which it can be used to correct is:

_____

_____

HOW TO BUILD SECURITY

Proper Investments Pay Big Dividends

As incongruous as it may seem, security rests not in the tangible things of the world but in the security that you are able to establish within your own mind. This does not mean that you disregard or discard such tangible evidences of security as you may possess, but rather that that which enables you to create and establish outer security is determined by your inner sense of security.

Who Is Secure?

For the most part people have been led to believe that security rests alone in what tangible assets they have been able to accumulate. If through some unforeseen cause these suddenly disappeared, many would give up and quit right now, feeling that there would be neither the time nor opportunity to build them up again — all is lost and that is all there is to it. On the other hand, there are those individuals who always seem to come out on top of any calamity better than they were before, regardless of age or circumstance. Some would call them lucky, but a closer scrutiny would reveal that their sense of security rested not in possessions but in the confidence in their own ability that, regardless of what happened, they *knew* that in some way, shape, or form everything would always be all right for them. They possessed a sense of security that had its foundations within themselves.

Security Available to All

This sense of inner security that some people have is available to everyone if he would go to the trouble of discovering what it actually means. Those who innately have it are not always aware that they have it, others develop it definitely and specifically, while

HOW TO BUILD SECURITY

still others labor at it and always seem to fall short. But there is a way to approach it that will always be productive of results, the degree depending upon the awareness of what it is.

What Is Security?

If true security rests within you, is an inner security, what must it encompass? You would first have to possess a feeling of security toward That which created you. You should realize that you were not created by chance and tossed into an inhospitable world to do the best you could, but that the Source of your being is continually active through you. You are not alone, but an individualization of the one creative Power. Your security rests only in the knowledge and acceptance of Life's continual activity in all your experience.

Continual Security

When you realize that That which once created your security is always active, and Its action is ever available to you in your experience, then you know that in spite of what might happen, what has once occurred for your benefit can occur again and in an even better way. Once you come to know that security rests not in tangible things but in That which is responsible for their appearance in your experience, then you will possess a sense of security that can never be disturbed by anything.

Creating Security

The one sure way of creating the experience of security that you desire is to know that God is the provider of all things, and that out of His limitless creative action comes an abundance of all good; that those things you have need of can be provided, are being provided, and always will be provided. If you do not accept your security in this manner you are denying what you think God to be and His beneficial action in your life. Regardless of what you might once have thought, final security rests in and flows from God, for all comes from this One Source.

HOW TO BUILD SECURITY

Accept What You Need

It is your thinking that makes available to you what you term your security. If, in spite of appearances, you are able to maintain a consistent pattern of thought that you will always possess a tangible security, and accept it as being your experience now, then there is no alternative but that out of the action of Life this is what is established for you. Any other form of security has no more stability than a castle of sand on the ocean shore; any tide of events can carry it away.

Sound Investments

The soundest investments you can make, which pay the surest and greatest dividends, are the thoughts you are able to implant firmly in your own mind that your security rests alone in the creative action of God. But the degree of tangible abundance that can be and is established in your experience is but a correspondence to your concept and acceptance of it. Security starts in your mind and heart; the ideas and emotions you possess are the deposits you make in the Bank of Life from which you may draw as liberally as you wish, according to the deposits you have made. Whether you have, or have not, depends upon you.

MENTAL STIMULANTS

SCIENCE: *The outside world of objects may thus be regarded as originating in a sustained mental field created by the Divine Mind—with which our minds are in a kind of rapport.*

—Raynor C. Johnson

PHILOSOPHY: *...if there be such a thing as ultimate reality in the universe, it must be something like ourselves: a Creative Mind, in which all things subsist.*

—Harris Elliott Kirk

RELIGION: *...seek ye the kingdom of God; and all these things shall be added unto you.*

—Luke 12:31

HOW TO BUILD SECURITY

THE DIET

Today and every day I know that I am always secure. That which created me has not forsaken me but is ever present and active in all aspects of my life and experience. It is through this infinite creative action that my every good need is continually fulfilled. I place my confidence and base my sense of security in this action, instead of in the results of the action. I am no longer satisfied only with results for I now have discovered That which is the cause of them. God is my partner throughout my experience of living and I now accept His abundance in all respects. My tangible security is but a reflection of the mental and emotional security I maintain. There is no questioning in my mind, no fear, and no anxiety, for I declare and accept that security in every sense is always mine. I have an unwavering and unshakable conviction that God can, does, and will always provide an abundance of all good things. Security *now* is mine to experience, not something to be sought for. The inner security I now know is the only real security and is the channel for the evidence of it in my life. With confidence I face the never-ending future in the wisdom that God always provides my every right need, right *now*.

— Capsule Supplement —

My final security is in God and His infinite creative action. I know that as I declare that security is ever present in my life, out of His limitless abundance that which I need for my security is always supplied.

o   o   o

Today I will apply this idea to these aspects of my thoughts and actions:

_____

_____

My particular problem, condition, or situation which it can be used to correct is:

_____

_____

LEARN TO LIKE YOURSELF

You Can't Avoid Living with Yourself

At some time or other you reach the point where you must have a certain amount of respect and consideration for yourself. You cannot get away from yourself, as much as you might sometimes like to. If the matter of living is to be an enjoyable experience the first person to get along with is yourself. The manner in which you regard yourself determines the manner in which you confront the world and the way it reacts to you. You are admonished to like others as you like yourself. Just how well do you like what you are?

Discover Some Good Qualities

Most people seem to have a perverse streak running through them that insists on emphasizing what they are *not* rather than what they *are;* they seem to dwell on their shortcomings, deficiencies, faults, and guilts. Remember, what you emphasize in your thinking tends to increase it. In spite of the ways in which you may seem lacking when you compare yourself with others, there is no person who cannot find within himself some good qualities in which he might excel. No, you are not perfect, nor could anyone ever hope to be, but that is no reason for you to concentrate on the negative rather than the positive qualities you possess.

Do Some Housecleaning

It could be a very good idea to examine in which ways you depreciate yourself. You accumulate a lot of notions about what you are as you go through life, which may or may not have any foundations in fact. But whether they do or not, you need to clean house and

LEARN TO LIKE YOURSELF

get rid of those ideas which do not contribute to a good opinion of what you are. After you eliminate all negative ideas you may or may not have much left, but whatever is left can be the foundation upon which to build that better person with whom you have to live. Start building a new concept, a new mental picture of that person you should be, a person that you would like.

Be Honest

This undertaking in no way involves developing a superiority complex or a sense of conceit. In fact, these are negative factors that have to be cleaned out just the same as any feelings of guilt, inadequacy, inability, resentment. Very few people have the courage to honestly evaluate the opinion they have of themselves. It is something no one likes to face. You may kid yourself by falsely overrating what you are, or, more generally, you may have too low an opinion of yourself. It is a difficult thing to do, but to the best of your ability you should honestly seek to discover wherein you wrongly estimate your worth.

One Starting Point

In seeking to build up a better and more wholesome opinion of yourself you have one point at which to start. You are alive and a creation of Life—God—and there is a reason and purpose in every expression of Life, and you are no exception. You are not a nobody, a lost soul, a worthless individual; these and other similar ideas you may have about yourself are purely figments of your imagination. Discard them and get back to the fundamental fact that Life is trying to achieve through you, and this It can and will do once you get rid of the limiting barriers you have established against Its action by the distorted opinions you may have about yourself.

Look in the Mirror

One important thing to do is to look in the mirror of your mind and see yourself as a person possessing admirable traits—a likeable character, a person with confidence in himself and certain of the nature and reason of his being. You begin to portray that role in

LEARN TO LIKE YOURSELF

your everyday experience. You are convinced that you are that person. This is not a matter of make-believe, for as you maintain this concept and act as though it were true, there is nothing that can prevent its becoming an actuality.

Thought Precedes Form

You need to remember that thought always tends to manifest itself in tangible form. So you cannot afford to have a low opinion of yourself, for that is the opinion others will have of you. If Divine Intelligence seeks to manifest Itself through the creation of *you*, you have no right to question the wisdom of that Intelligence. Rather, it becomes necessary for you to discover within yourself those things which It ever seeks to become through you.

Don't Deny Yourself

You cannot resign from Life. Do not violate God's concept of you by trying to minimize yourself. Come to like what you *really* are, learn to live with yourself in joy and happiness. Negative ideas about yourself will diminish and finally disappear as you establish in their place a loftier opinion which expresses the nature of the infinite Spirit at the center of your being.

MENTAL STIMULANTS

SCIENCE: *...God seems to be giving to man a spark of His own Intelligence.*

—A. Cressy Morrison

PHILOSOPHY: *Courage, then, for God works in you. In the order of time you embody in outer acts what is for him the truth of his eternity.*

—Josiah Royce

RELIGION: *...he that keepeth his commandments dwelleth in him, and he in him. And hereby we know that he abideth in us, by the Spirit which he hath given us.*

—I John 3:24

LEARN TO LIKE YOURSELF

THE DIET

Today I know that, the same as every other person, I am a purposeful and creative expression of the activity of Life which ever seeks to find greater fulfillment in Its creation. I no longer minimize God or Life by minimizing myself. Instead, I ever seek to discover and express the nature and qualities of That which created me. I come to love myself because I appreciate the Life within me, and I give thanks for Its vital, dynamic expression as what I am. I know myself to be a wonderful person, and through this knowing this is the kind of person I become. As I come to like myself for what I really am, dismissing all derogatory ideas, Life takes on new meaning. To the degree that I like myself I am now able to like others. Without conceit or any sense of superiority, but with awe and admiration, I now recognize and accept myself as the fulfillment of a Divine idea, an idea of power, beauty, joy, and creativity. I now permit this idea to fully express itself as the wonderful person I am.

— Capsule Supplement —

I now know that, regardless of what I may have considered myself to be in the past, at the center of my being I am a wonderful expression of an idea in the Mind of God. This is what I ever seek to more fully express in all my thoughts and acts.

o o o

Today I will apply this idea to these aspects of my thoughts and actions:

_____

_____

My particular problem, condition, or situation which it can be used to correct is:

_____

_____

DISCOVER YOUR PLACE IN LIFE

There Is a Need for Your Abilities

You possess certain abilities which you need to recognize and seek to capitalize on. In many instances certain abilities just naturally blossom forth. At other times you may seek to discover what new capabilities you might possess and then cultivate and develop them. In any situation, or in whatever direction you may think you are best able to give to the world of what you have, there is a proper place for you to do so.

Source of Your Abilities

In order to find your proper place in life in relation to what you have to contribute, it is first necessary that you have a firm understanding of the nature and source of your abilities. Fundamentally, Life is an active, constructive, and purposeful endeavor and this activity and purpose do not end with the creation of you, but of necessity must continue through what you are and do. Life has something to express and create through you. You have been graced with intelligence, an individualization of the infinite Intelligence, and it is up to you to recognize this and do something about it.

Interrelationships

Although at times nature may seem to be wasteful and overextravagant, closer examination will disclose that there is a reason and purpose in all things. At some point and in some way everything is to a degree dependent on everything else. In this light it can be seen that whatever it is in which you can excel there is a right place and a right way for you to do it.

DISCOVER YOUR PLACE IN LIFE

You Have Something to Offer

Often in your work and activities you may feel that you are not allowed to contribute the best of your abilities and as a result do nothing that enables you to have a sense of being creative. Regardless of what work you are engaged in, in some way you need to find within yourself something that you can contribute to it, whether the endeavor is entirely to your liking or not.

Start Contributing

A possible key to finding the proper place or activity for the release of your abilities is always to contribute. New ways and means of using your abilities will never develop unless you make use of every possible opportunity to offer something of what you are in all that you do. Unless you learn to do this, and do it with joy and enthusiasm, you may find that you inhibit the creative flow of Life through you and become an automaton doing just those things necessary to keep yourself alive. You were not created for this type of existence.

Enjoy What You Are Doing

Regardless of how high a goal you may have set for yourself, or how lowly your present activity may be in relationship to it, a negative attitude will prevent you from finding a better outlet for your abilities. Only when you are able to contribute to your present activity will it become a steppingstone to something that enables you to do more. And whether you feel that you have a lot or a little to contribute, there are always those untapped inner resources which may be called upon.

Your Right Place

There is a right place for you in the scheme of things, a place that will provide you with the proper outlets for your abilities and at the same time offer you the proper recompense. However frustrated or resentful you may be at the present time, it is necessary that you discard such feelings and always contribute your best. If you establish a pattern of thinking that you are always in the wrong place it usually works out that this is always

DISCOVER YOUR PLACE IN LIFE

where you will be. On the other hand, if you consider each day's endeavor a challenge to give the best you have, you will find that this is the best and fastest way to find better opportunities for the fuller expression of your creative abilities.

Act Today

Today is the only time you can express more of the Life that flows through you. Start now to give, to the best of your ability, to your every activity, whether it be digging a ditch, running a big corporation, or managing a home. Life is always waiting for you to permit It to flow more fully through your activities, and there is always a right place, a right way, and a purposeful reason for what It can contribute to Itself through you.

MENTAL STIMULANTS

SCIENCE: *A rich and full personality, in moral and spiritual harmony with itself and with its destiny, one whose talents are not buried in a napkin, and whose wholeness transcends its conflicts, is the highest creation of which we have knowledge, and in its attainment the individual possibilities of the evolutionary process are brought to supreme fruition.*

—Julian Huxley

PHILOSOPHY: *...I have no doubt that the great Accomplisher of Creation is directing within me with a single-minded purpose an inward awakening in spite of all obstructions, and in spite of my own contradictions.*

—Rabindranath Tagore

RELIGION: *And God is able to make all grace abound toward you; that ye, always having all sufficiency in all things, may abound to every good work.*

—II Corinthians 9:8

DISCOVER YOUR PLACE IN LIFE

THE DIET

I know that in the Mind of God there is a reason and a purpose to be fulfilled through my life. I continually seek the greater potentials which reside within me, knowing that as I recognize them, accept them, and express them, there is a right way and a right place for this creative activity. All frustrations and resentments about what I am now doing are discarded for I know that there are proper outlets for whatever abilities I possess and express. In all that I undertake I discover what it is of myself that I can contribute to my endeavor. I am never at a loss as to what to say or do that can in some way enhance all that I undertake. Today I know that I am in my right place, and I rightfully give to it the best that I have. My right place tomorrow may not be the same as today's, for as I increasingly permit the creative expression of Life through me, ever greater opportunities open up to me. I know that my way is made clear, that I am guided and directed in a manner that permits me to express to the utmost the innermost nature of my being. I continually find myself in my right place, and the reciprocal action of Life properly returns to me an abundance in proportion to what I give to It.

— Capsule Supplement —

I know that God is continually active and creative through me and that there is a unique purpose for my being. I discover my rightful place in life so that I may give the best of what I am.

o   o   o

Today I will apply this idea to these aspects of my thoughts and actions:

_____

_____

My particular problem, condition, or situation which it can be used to correct is:

_____

_____

PEACE OF MIND CAN BE YOURS

The Value of Being Discontented

There has been a lot of talk and a lot written about "peace of mind." Some seem to think that it is something to be desired and others say that they want nothing to do with it. Apparently there is considerable misunderstanding as to just what it means. As a place to start you might consider peace of mind as the absence of confusion and conflict in your thinking.

Harmonious Action

With this approach to the subject you can discover that peace of mind involves harmonious action. It should not mean complacency, inaction, nor a state of vacuous living in which nothing ever happens. Living involves the solving of problems, the overcoming of difficulties, and the achievement of worthwhile goals, and none of these things can be accomplished with a state of mind that is confused or chaotic. Rather, there needs to be a peaceful activity within the mind, an orderly, creative, constructive activity which is able to face and adequately meet the challenge of living.

Your Need To Accomplish

Life is action, not lack of it, and this action is orderly and purposeful. Peace of mind can only be achieved when you are active and productive. Within you there is ever the urge, which you cannot avoid, to actively participate in living. It has been referred to as a Divine discontent, a never-ending urge to be more of what you are. Perhaps wrong definitions have been given to peace and contentment. Perhaps such emotions and feelings do not relate to a state of existence but to the satisfaction gained from things accomplished.

PEACE OF MIND CAN BE YOURS

Avoid Complacency

You may think that you need complete complacency, a complete lack of challenge of things to be done. But if you achieve this you will find yourself in such a morass of boredom that there will be nothing to live for nor have peace of mind about. The active person is the happy person—the person who seems at peace with himself and his world, even though his activities involve challenges to his abilities. A peaceful existence cannot permit of inaction, for where there is inaction there is no life.

Start To Live

You are born to be active and peace of mind comes from the satisfaction that you are doing something worthwhile, in spite of any difficulties or problems that may confront you in the process. This means that you must get over resenting the challenges that you meet and instead welcome them as opportunities for greater achievement. The extent to which you are able to start to live in such a manner rests on your ability to rid your thoughts of confusion and conflict.

Remove Inner Conflicts

The great disrupting and inhibiting factor in attaining peace of mind is the confusion of your own thoughts. The successful person, the happy person, is the one who knows what he knows, so there is no chaos, conflict, or confusion in what he thinks and believes. A specific and firm foundation is needed if harmonious action is to be established in your life. The only source for such a foundation is the recognition that your mind is an individualization of the infinite Mind. When you are able to convince yourself of this, then you can also permit yourself to accept the harmony that must of necessity be Its nature.

Peace Starts at Home

The starting place for harmonious activity in your life and experience is within the pattern of your own thinking. Once you establish in your thought the idea that you are no longer confused, no longer in conflict with yourself, then you may begin to look about you for the evidence of the harmony that has come to exist in your own mind. The peace you

PEACE OF MIND CAN BE YOURS

desire you must first create and accept within your thought. Once this is done, then regardless of where you may be—at home, the office, traveling, or with friends—the peace you know through the lack of conflict and confusion of your own thinking surrounds you at all times.

Discover Contentment

There is one thing that you should never forget: Contentment can only spring from a discontent with things as they are, which in turn resolves itself into a peaceful satisfaction for things achieved as the result of a dynamic, creative activity on your part. Peace of mind means orderly action; the opposite is disorder and chaos. The peace of mind that the world needs will not come from "happiness pills" but from stimulating, dynamic, and creative thinking.

MENTAL STIMULANTS

SCIENCE: *...the thing that really started and maintains progress in the world is man's ability to think, and his dissatisfaction with things as they are. That is the tangible* motive power *which makes for human progress.*
—Charles F. Kettering

PHILOSOPHY: *It is within my power either to serve God, or not to serve Him. Serving Him I add to my own good and the good of the whole world. Not serving Him, I forfeit my own good and deprive the world of that good, which was in my power to create.*
—Leo Tolstoy

RELIGION: *Thou believest that there is one God; thou doest well....But wilt thou know...that faith without works is dead?*
—James 2:19-20

PEACE OF MIND CAN BE YOURS

THE DIET

I welcome the discontent that continually wells up from within me, for I recognize it as the Divine urge to express the purposeful activity of Life. I welcome the challenges, the problems, the difficulties that I may encounter, for living involves a continual endeavor, a constant aspiration, a never-ending goal to be achieved. I seek neither to escape nor retire from active participation in living. Instead, I invite and accept from infinite Intelligence a greater desire and ability to express Its active nature. As I do this all confusion and conflict within my thought disappear, and harmonious, orderly thinking takes over. I now find joy, peace, and happiness in all that I do and in all of my surroundings, for my thoughts now reflect the nature of God's thoughts and they are productive of harmonious action and satisfaction. I do not rest in a false peace, but ever seek to discover that true joy which comes with a full and active participation in the dynamic and purposeful creativity of Life. Peace of mind is now mine, for I know that it is the satisfaction that comes from the successful completion of a creative act and a contribution to Life.

— Capsule Supplement —

I discover that true peace of mind, devoid of conflict and confusion, which comes with actively fulfilling my place in life. I permit myself to be a channel for the creative activity of God which never ceases.

o o o

Today I will apply this idea to these aspects of my thoughts and actions:

_____

_____

My particular problem, condition, or situation which it can be used to correct is:

_____

_____

USING THE POWER OF LOVE

Love Alone Makes Life Worthwhile

It could be said that the most important single thing in your experiencing of a more worthwhile life is your capacity to love. Love has been described as the greatest thing in the world, a force that cannot be resisted and that establishes peace and harmony. You are probably so used to hearing songs about it, and reading what the poets have said, that for the most part you have failed to recognize the important practical benefits of love in your daily life.

The Necessity of Love

To establish and maintain a mental and emotional attitude of love is essential in every aspect of your life. You are never devoid of a reaction to a person or situation, and when you are not capable of having a favorable attitude you find yourself with one which contains resentment, hate, and dislike. Love alone is a constructive factor; all contrary to it is destructive. When you lack love you are denying yourself the very thing that you say you most desire—a more worthwhile life. Actually, you have no choice as to whether you shall love, it is a matter of necessity for without it every aspect of your experience deteriorates.

The Nature of Love

It has been pointed out that love is fundamentally a recognition of the interdependence of all things and the realization that there must be cooperative relationships. The dynamic force of love goes far beyond the intimate relationship between man and woman, beautiful and sublime as it is. It applies to the harmony that must exist between all parts

USING THE POWER OF LOVE

of life—family, neighbors, associates, states, and nations. There is no undertaking of man that can deprive itself of the action of love without suffering the effects of its detrimental opposites. Love alone provides harmony, constructive endeavor, and mutual well-being.

Physical Aspects

What many people do not realize is the vital importance of an attitude of love on their physical well-being. There is practically no function of the body that cannot be adversely affected by its lack. Conversely, the person who is able to embody a feeling of love in every respect finds that his body functions in a more harmonious manner.

Mental Aspects

Equally obvious is the effect of a lack of love on the way you think. When hatred and animosity, instead of love, fill your mind there is turmoil, confusion, and lack of constructive thinking. When intense dislike is uppermost in your thought it becomes an obsession and dominates everything you do and say in a negative manner. On the other hand, a mental attitude of love permits of orderly and constructive processes of thought. Dissatisfaction with your present state of affairs can urge you on to greater achievement, but when you permit this dissatisfaction to grow into hatred, then you will find that your thinking is so distorted that creative endeavor is impossible.

Love Is a Magnet

You must never overlook the fact that any feeling contrary to a sense of love is depriving you of the things you would like the most. Those emotions you strongly feel have the ability to draw into your experience their tangible counterparts. Whether such feelings concern situations, conditions, or people, you will only be able to find in your experience a reflection of the way you feel. The important thing is not to struggle against undesirable experiences which evidence a lack of expressions of love, but instead remold them by remolding your thought so that it is a complete embodiment of love. You start with yourself to change the world about you. Like does beget like.

USING THE POWER OF LOVE

Love Is Essential

The person who is not loved or who seems incapable of loving soon finds that hi life begins to wither away. For your physical and mental welfare you must develop the capa ity to love, because if you don't you not only deprive yourself but others of the benefit of this constructive power. Love may be said to be an essential aspect of all living thing and if you fail to incorporate it in your living you cut yourself off from Life.

Gro ing Up

The capacity to increase your experience of the benefits of love is a never-ending p ss. You have to start removing every big and little negative attitude you can discover w u n yourself. You start being constructive rather than adding to what you already n ght dislike. The greatest constructive creative force is love, and you can use this power to remold, transform, and renew your whole experience in living.

MENTAL STIMULANTS

SCIENCE: *Love is the universal creative force.... Love replaces the struggle for existence by harmonious and mutual aid.*
— Pitirim A. Sorokin

PHILOSOPHY: *Love is the...substantial bond...between...the universal and the in li- vidual, the divine and the human. Love is God himself, and apart f n it there is no God. Love makes man God and God man.*
— Ludwig F uerbach

RELIGION: *...by love serve one another. For all the law is fulfilled in one word, even in this; Thou shalt love thy neighbour as thyself.*
— Galatians 5:13 14

USING THE POWER OF LOVE

THE DIET

All is the creation of the harmonious action of God, an expression of God's Love. It is in this Love that I live, move, and have my being. I now declare that in everything I am and do I accept a greater influx and outflow of the Love that is God. As I love, I am loved. As I help another, I am helped. My whole life is filled with a sense of love for all people. My way is made clear, my cup runneth over, my body is made whole, and my experiences are happy through the creative power of the God-like love that I express in all ways. The love I express brings joy to others and returns to me, making my life worthwhile. Regardless of what confronts me I meet the situation with the creative, constructive force of Love which makes all things right. The Love that is God, the great motivating Power of all life, I recognize as actively renewing and transforming every aspect of my experience. Love alone rules my life.

—Capsule Supplement—

Love—harmony, cooperation, and mutual assistance—is the very foundation of my life. In my every thought, emotion, and action I express only Love, and this Divine Power makes everything right in my world.

✿   ✿   ✿

Today I will apply this idea to these aspects of my thoughts and actions:

_____

_____

My particular problem, condition, or situation which it can be used to correct is:

_____

_____

THE
FOURTH
WEEK

During the next seven days the mental diet presents ideas which can have a beneficial influence on your health. Wisely used, they can help you regain what you may have lost, or enable you to keep what you already have.

WHY YOU SHOULD BE HEALTHY • LEARN TO AVOID STRESS AND ANXIETY

HOW TO INSURE YOUR HEALTH • WAYS TO INCREASE YOUR VITALITY

YOU CAN AVOID OLD AGE • STOP BEING SICK

ENJOY NEW HEALTH AND HAPPINESS

WHY YOU SHOULD BE HEALTHY

It's the Normal, Natural Way To Be

In spite of the way you may now feel, or the way you may have felt on some yester-day, the basic fact remains that it is in the nature of things that the life you live should be healthy and that every function and action of your body should be perfect. This is not a matter of blinding yourself to the evidence, but rather of looking at the actual facts!

Facts About Health

You may seem to be swamped with various aches and pains, ailments of one kind or another, all of which vary in their severity. You may have reached the point where you have accepted such conditions as being what life is, something to be suffered through. But how wrong can you be! By what right have you declared that life is a sickly and ailing affair? Any doctor or scientist who deals with the life processes will confirm the fact that, of necessity, expressions of life, fundamentally, should be perfect. If this were not the case living things would have disappeared from the face of the earth long ago! If living things had not been able to fight off invading diseases, to maintain the normal, natural functioning of all the parts of the body, to renew and reconstruct damaged parts, they would never have gotten beyond even the one-cell stage.

Health Comes from Within

In spite of the great confidence you may have in doctors and their amazing ability to assist you in times of physical difficulty, it is the body that heals itself. Assistance may

WHY YOU SHOULD BE HEALTHY

be provided, obstacles removed, and certain mechanical things done, but in the last analysis the doctor sits back and waits for the normal activity of the body to take over and re-establish healthy functioning.

The Source of Health

If health is the normal natural condition of your body, what is its source? What is it that determines what the norm shall be, and why does it maintain itself? Research has revealed many interesting things about how the body functions, but as to the "why" very little has been said. Some outstanding scientists have stated that the body exhibits a dynamic quality, which indicates that there is some intelligent purpose, some creative organizing force that guides, directs, and maintains it in a stable state of health.

God Is Life

This force or intelligence inherent in every living thing is immaterial, a spiritual Power which maintains a perfect pattern of what things should be. Although all expressions of Life are unique, and no two are alike, there is a pattern, a form, a mold to which each adheres and by which it is maintained. It is an idea in the Mind of God that has made you, maintains you, and renews you, and this idea of necessity has to embody perfection.

What Happened?

But what about your aches and pains? They are very concrete, definite, and not to your liking—or so you say. Excluding accidents and massive invasion by infection, what happens to you when you encounter ill-health? It would appear that in some way you have obstructed or inhibited the action of the perfect, purposeful organizing Life-Force which manifests Itself in you. How can you do this? If this creative action within you is an expression of infinite Intelligence, then it would appear that a misdirection of Its action likely could only result from another form of thought—your own!

Healthy Thinking

This to a large extent places the matter of the state of your own health right on your own doorstep, just where you don't want it! There is no separation between your mind

WHY YOU SHOULD BE HEALTHY

and your body. They are but different aspects of the creative action of Life and you are a unified whole. It is your ability to think that can lead you into experiences of ill-health. Recognition of this fact has been known for ages and has recently given birth to that branch of medicine known as psychosomatics. Healthy thoughts are necessary before you can have a healthy body. You have to learn to think in terms of health!

You Are Healthy

In straightening out your thinking relative to your health you must first reach the conviction that at the very center Life is perfect. You must know that you are intended to be healthy and that Life can and will manifest health in you as you permit It to do so. Cease thinking in terms of any illness you might have, or what dire thing could happen to you, for these are the thoughts that inhibit health and become creative of the conditions you do not want to experience. You can maintain your health, or regain it, once you know that it is always available to you as your natural, normal state, and cease establishing through your thoughts conditions contrary to it.

MENTAL STIMULANTS

SCIENCE: *...there is no aspect of the body system which isn't influenced by the brain's efforts to adapt, and...bodily processes changed by mental activity may lead to serious physical damage.*
                                            —American Medical Association Report

PHILOSOPHY: *As a man thinketh, so is he, and as a man chooseth, so is he and so is nature.*
                                            —Ralph Waldo Emerson

RELIGION: *Be ye therefore perfect, even as your Father which is in heaven is perfect.*
                                            —Matthew 5:48

WHY YOU SHOULD BE HEALTHY

THE DIET

There is One Life, that Life is God, that Life is perfect, and that Life is my life now. In this knowledge I know that it is normal, right, and natural that my body in every respect should manifest perfect health. Every cell, every organ, every function is now as it should be. There is perfect circulation, assimilation, and elimination. That Divine idea which created my body now maintains, sustains, and renews every aspect of it. What does not belong is discarded, what needs to be repaired is now being made whole. I let loose of all my fears and apprehensions about my health and what might happen to me, and accept the creative action of infinite Intelligence which manifests as all life. It knows what to do, how to do it, and is doing it right now in Its manifestation as my body. Health is not a nebulous idea but a Divine fact. Perfection always exists in the Mind of God and I accept and declare that this perfection is manifesting in me now. God created me and His Intelligence now makes perfect His creation. I accept health as the normal state of my being, and this alone is what becomes my experience.

— Capsule Supplement —

There is One Life, that Life is God, that Life is perfect, and that Life is my life now. The intelligent, purposeful activity of Life is now freely manifesting Its wholeness in every part of my body.

❂ ❂ ❂

Today I will apply this idea to these aspects of my thoughts and actions:

_____

_____

My particular problem, condition, or situation which it can be used to correct is:

_____

_____

LEARN TO AVOID STRESS AND ANXIETY

You Create Your Problems

Today's living seems to be filled with stress, anxiety, and pressure. Everybody, in one way or another, apparently suffers from being alive in our present civilization. Although the causes of such conditions may exist in the world about you, you alone determine how you are going to react to them. You have the privilege of allowing conditions around you to become the cause of problems within you, or to rise above them.

Mind and Body

It has been ascertained that the mental reactions you have to conditions about you are responsible for specific bodily reactions. The longer a sustained adverse mental reaction is maintained the more severe will become the body's reaction, and eventually you can find yourself with a serious health problem. In other words, your sustained negative mental attitudes can and do become tangible as disease. Medical chronicles are filled with illustrations of the way the process occurs. The body has no choice but to correspond in nature and function to the quality of your thoughts and emotions.

No One Is Exempt

If there is one thing you cannot do it is to divorce your body from the body of your thought. Simple illustrations of the way the heart beats faster as a result of a sense of fear, the way the stomach becomes upset with feelings of hate, and the manner in which the intestines behave with emotional extremes, all point out the unity of your being.

LEARN TO AVOID STRESS AND ANXIETY

These are obvious occurrences, but there are many others which you are not so aware of, and all too often extreme damage could be done before you realize the detrimental nature of the negative mental sprees you may indulge in.

Don't Stop Living

You cannot avoid the various problems that arise in the course of daily living. They are part and parcel of life and are to be squarely faced and adequately met. But in the process you must always be alert to dealing with the situation objectively and not literally swallowing the problem and letting it create havoc within you. You have to learn to keep things in their proper places. If you let an external problem develop into an internal problem of an ulcer you have gained nothing, but now you have two problems instead of one. The answer is not a matter of avoiding life, but of dealing with it in a healthy manner.

The Place for Problems

The problems you encounter in your daily experience are external to you. Leave them there! You can deal with them much better if they are out where you can see them, properly appraise them, and determine an adequate course of action. However, once you bring them into yourself you find your mind becomes a turmoil, your emotions erratic, and your body begins to malfunction. When you realize that your mind, an individualization of the One Mind, can transcend any negative experience you might encounter, then you have a starting place for properly dealing with whatever problem you have; you approach it with the constructive tools of thought which can correct it.

Life Is Interesting

What makes life interesting is the challenges that you encounter. A state of continual bliss would be intolerable. You have your ups and downs, your joys and heartaches. Variety is necessary for an interest in living. But it is the negative extremes you need to avoid, and particularly those that you maintain for a long period of time. Life is to be enjoyed, but you will never have a chance to enjoy it if you let yourself wallow in a bog of stress, anxiety, and pressure. These reactions are vital and necessary so that you may do and be the best that you are, but you cannot allow them to run wild.

LEARN TO AVOID STRESS AND ANXIETY

Work with Yourself

There are many pills and potions on the market today for minimizing or relieving extreme reactions to the stresses and strains of living, and in some instances they have worked wonders. But they mostly seem to be of little value in correcting the external problem or the individual's basic ability to properly meet it. The ability to live a normal healthy life, without the adverse influences of destructive emotional reactions, rests in what you can do about the way you think. To properly face a problem situation you must first face yourself.

Enjoyable Living

If you can come to accept that Mind, in Its infinite wisdom, knows what to do about the situation in which you are involved; that you are rightly guided and directed in what you do and say relative to it; and also that Its individualization as your mind permits of no destructive reaction, then you can relax with a calm mental assurance and an emotional stability that will permit you to live as you should live.

MENTAL STIMULANTS

SCIENCE: *But whether he puts his faith in God or in creation, man realizes that his ultimate aim must outlast the moment ... [this] should lead us through a meaningful, happy, active, and long life, steering us clear of the unpleasant and unnecessary stresses of fights, frustrations, and insecurities.*

—Hans Selye

PHILOSOPHY: *Faith is the basis of our present world and lack of faith the source of our discords.*

—Ralph Tyler Flewelling

RELIGION: *...whatsoever is born of God overcometh the world: and this is the victory that overcometh the world, even our faith.*

—I John 5:4

LEARN TO AVOID STRESS AND ANXIETY

THE DIET

I face life with calm assurance, a feeling of strength and security, that enables me to discover a new-found joy. Gone are the damaging stresses, anxieties, and pressures I formerly experienced, for I know that the Life that is at the center of my being knows nothing of these things and It now guides and directs me in all that I do. Mental turmoil, emotional imbalance, and physical disturbances cease to be part of my experience, for I know them to be no part of God, whose Life I now accept as my life. I handle all things that need to be taken care of in an enthusiastic manner that is creative and good. All that is to be done in my daily life I do with ease and joy. With confidence I know that God, to whom all things are known, makes known to me the proper thing to do at the proper time. I do not avoid living, but enter into living more enthusiastically, for I know that the more I express Life the more It expresses Itself in wholeness and completeness in me. I start to live anew—new in mind, new in feeling, and new in body.

— Capsule Supplement —

In God there is only good. There are no opposites—irritations, stresses, or strains. I now accept God as the Source of my life, and experience only harmony in my daily living.

✿　✿　✿

Today I will apply this idea to these aspects of my thoughts and actions:

_____

_____

My particular problem, condition, or situation which it can be used to correct is:

_____

_____

HOW TO INSURE YOUR HEALTH

It's Never Too Late To Protect Yourself

There are a great many things involved in being healthy and staying healthy. Fundamental, of course, is the requisite of common sense in the care, treatment, and feeding of your body. Once you have done all that can be done physically for the proper care of your body, you then want some kind of insurance that guarantees health will be maintained.

The Cost of Health Insurance

The insurance of your health demands that a high price be paid. The effect of the nature of your thinking on the condition of your body is a well-established fact, so you find yourself at the point where you have to deal with what you are thinking. It is a very definite challenge to think consistently, particularly in a constructive manner. When you are ill it is easy to think of nothing but your illness, but whether you are either sick or well, how much time are you able to devote to thinking in terms of health? It is not easy, but it is only through your ability to maintain a pattern of thought that embodies health that you are able to maintain or regain health. For this, effort is required, but it is a key to what you desire.

The Effectiveness of Thought

It has been ascertained that when a person is sick the effectiveness of a medication he may be taking rests to a large extent on how effective the individual thinks it will be. Sometimes certain antibiotics, which are usually 100% effective for specific conditions, are useless as a result of the patient's attitude toward them. At other times sugar pills, placebos,

HOW TO INSURE YOUR HEALTH

can have the effect of antibiotics if the patient thinks they will be that effective. This would indicate that, sick or well, the changes that might and can occur in a person's body are controlled or influenced by what he is thinking.

Examine Yourself

Whether you are sick or well, it is of vital importance that you give yourself a health examination. Take the time to discover what it is that you are thinking about your health the majority of the time. You may discover that you are guaranteeing your illness rather than your health. In most instances it will be found that much will have to be done before you can supply yourself with adequate health insurance, insurance that nobody and nothing else can supply.

Insurance Payments

When you feel well, do you ever take the time to acknowledge the fact that you feel well, to be grateful for good health, and to know that health is the normal, natural way for you to be? It is necessary that you keep such thoughts firmly established. This is the way you make your health insurance payments. Even if you are now ill, payments of this kind—the daily consistent thinking about the health that is rightfully yours—will gradually build up a deposit to your credit which will re-establish what you have temporarily lost. Your every thought about either health or ill-health is a payment toward what you will experience. Have you been making the right kind of payments lately?

Body Response

The body cannot help but respond to the nature of what you are thinking. In this connection it has also been found that what a doctor thinks about the condition of his patient does have an effect on what occurs. For this reason it has been suggested that the doctor should watch his thinking carefully so as not to adversely affect the patient. If it is important for a doctor to be careful about what he thinks about his patient, how much more important it is that you be careful about what you think about yourself.

HOW TO INSURE YOUR HEALTH

It Is Never Too Late

It is never too late nor too soon to start to think about yourself in terms of health. If you are healthy now, through a firmly established pattern of thinking about health, you can maintain it. On the other hand, thought being an immediately creative thing, can, when properly directed, literally revitalize a person even when he seems to be drawing his last breath. To be healthy and to stay healthy you have to have a concept of health in your mind.

The Future

The health insurance you start creating today can make all your tomorrows happy ones. But there is the requirement that you continue to make your payments regularly and be certain that the payments are of the kind that will purchase the insurance you want. Every thought can be said to be a purchase of an experience. Life is the supplier of health, but you can have it only as you buy it—buy it with continual payments of thoughts of health.

MENTAL STIMULANTS

SCIENCE: *It is obvious that when a man is well, he is well in mind and body. When he is sick, he is more than likely to be sick in mind and body, too.*
—Flanders Dunbar

PHILOSOPHY: *...just as you mustn't try to heal the eyes without the head or the head without the body, so neither must you try to heal the body without the soul.*
—Plato

RELIGION: *Why art thou cast down, O my soul? and why art thou disquieted within me? hope thou in God: for I shall yet praise him, who is the health of my countenance, and my God.*
—Psalm 42:11

HOW TO INSURE YOUR HEALTH

THE DIET

Everything that God has made is good, it could not be otherwise. In a universe that is intelligent, constructive, and purposeful my experience of normal, natural health is my rightful state. I know that health is always mine to experience and that it is always available to me in accordance with my acceptance of it. I continually accept health in my every thought and emotion. As I maintain health in my mind, that is what I experience in my body. I now free myself from any tendency on my part, or that of others, to say that health is not mine. I build my health, I maintain my health, thought by thought, and nothing can deter me in my acceptance of the perfection of the One Life as active and creative in and through me. I remove all ideas of fear and anxiety about my body and leave it free to perfectly manifest its perfect pattern—an idea in the Mind of God. Infinite Intelligence governs all the functions of my body and as I keep my own thinking clear and receptive to Its action, health is mine. Today and every day I insure God's gift of health to me by the healthy pattern of my thinking, which permits nothing unlike it to be entertained in my mind or body.

— Capsule Supplement —

I am healthy, and I remain healthy, through my knowledge that what God creates is good. I accept health as my normal state and insure its continuance by discarding all thoughts to the contrary.

❂   ❂   ❂

Today I will apply this idea to these aspects of my thoughts and actions:

_____

_____

My particular problem, condition, or situation which it can be used to correct is:

_____

_____

WAYS TO INCREASE
YOUR VITALITY

Start to Use Your Resources

Perhaps, too often, you complain of tiredness, weariness, exhaustion, lack of vitality, and of feeling low physically. This of course could not possibly be the way you should normally feel, although you may have established such a condition as your regular state of affairs. Daily living does have a cycle, a period of activity followed by a period of rest. But to be tired all the time without activity, or to be unduly exhausted with a minimum of effort, would indicate that something needs to be done. You need to discover the source of your vitality and make use of it.

Causes of Tiredness

Even though you may have what the doctors would say is a normal healthy body, this is no assurance that you feel vital and alive. When you are bogged down physically and don't feel like doing anything, you seldom have to look far to find the cause. When your thinking has no stimulus, when you are bored, when you lack a vital interest, your body reacts in a similar manner. The functioning of the organs becomes sluggish, you seem to have no strength in your muscles, and the whole vital process of your body slows down.

The Source of Vitality

The vitality of either the mind or the body first rests in the nature of Life. It is always dynamic, purposeful, and constructive, and as It is the source of what you are, the vitality that you may and should possess is Its uninhibited flow through you. Due to the unity of mind and body, the mind may limit the vitality of the body, which in turn appears to affect the vitality of the mind.

WAYS TO INCREASE YOUR VITALITY

Learn To Be Sharp

When you are aware of the fact that lack of bodily vitality stems from an unstimulating pattern of thinking, it is time that you start to pull yourself up by your bootstraps. You have to use your thoughts to correct your thoughts. Regardless of how bogged down mentally you may feel, you must of necessity recognize that you are still a part of Life; that It is all that It ever was, and that It is inspiring and stimulating your thoughts. Life is always expressing Itself, always seeking a greater channel for Its flow through you. You need to open your mind to Its influx, consciously and deliberately, and develop an eagerness for the new things that It can become through you.

Physical Stimulus

Mentally knowing and accepting that the body is alive and vital paves the way for it to become so. Any degree to which you may be able to acknowledge that Life in all Its fullness is increasingly active within you, to that degree will your body respond and then you will be able to affirm it to an even greater degree. No thought is an idle thought, but each and every one does have an effect that corresponds to it. You can vitalize your thought to stimulate your body, and you also can use thought to further stimulate your thinking.

Necessity of Action

Action is the essence of Life. Action is also the essence of thought. Nothing can happen unless there is prior cause of some kind. The vitality you possess is an indication of the amount of Life you are accepting and permitting yourself to experience. For a healthy, vital body you must establish active, vital patterns of thinking.

Overcoming Barriers

In a great many instances you may have erected barriers which you refuse to remove so that you can become more vital and alive. You have built a wall about you which cuts

WAYS TO INCREASE YOUR VITALITY

you off from living. As hesitant and reluctant as you may be to break out of your state of hibernation, you must in some way endeavor to start to tear down the wall. You literally have to force yourself to start to be active and creative in some way, regardless of how small a way it may be at first. The Life within you must find expression through you, and once you give It any sort of opportunity you will find that you will break out of your shell and start to express the person you fundamentally are.

Vitality Unlimited

All the strength, vitality, wisdom, enthusiasm, and joy there is or can be already exists. It is only a matter of accepting them as your experience. It is a simple thing to do, but not necessarily easy. Your only source, and only resource, for any new situation resides in the nature and action of Mind, Intelligence, God. Your vitality is there in unlimited abundance, so unlimit your thinking, free your body of the restrictions you have imposed on it, and start to *live*.

MENTAL STIMULANTS

SCIENCE: *Science today confirms what religion has intuitively known from time immemorial, that faith, love, and hope can work miracles of healing and restoration.*
— Joseph H. Krimsky

PHILOSOPHY: *Thou art thyself a fragment torn from God. Thou hast a portion of Him within thyself.*
— Epictetus

RELIGION: *God is my strength and power: and he maketh my way perfect.*
— II Samuel 22:33

WAYS TO INCREASE YOUR VITALITY

THE DIET

I know that there is unlimited vitality available to me for my every good undertaking. The strength and power of the One Life animates every part of my being. Every part of my body is stimulated to a normal activity, and a new surge of well-being floods through me. There is in my mind no thought that can in any way hinder this action, for I now accept Life and no longer deny or refuse Its flow through me. My knowing and accepting that this is taking place clears away all obstacles to Life's action. I never lack the mental or physical strength to do that which I need to do to accomplish the good I desire. I keep my thoughts healthy and refuse to contaminate them with ideas detrimental to my bodily health. My body is a mirror of my mind and I let my mind be a mirror of the One Mind. I turn to Life at the center of my being and now affirm that It flows freely through my mind and body, instilling vitality, enthusiasm, creativeness, and right action. God is my life and strength, is what I am, and this is the life I start living today.

— Capsule Supplement —

The life and vitality of God is my life. I discard all ideas to the contrary and accept and affirm that in every way, in mind and body, there is a dynamic flow of Divine vitality through me which makes my living a joyful experience.

✿ ✿ ✿

Today I will apply this idea to these aspects of my thoughts and actions:

_____

_____

My particular problem, condition, or situation which it can be used to correct is:

_____

_____

YOU CAN AVOID OLD AGE
You Are as Old as You Think You Are

For all practical purposes it is the nature of your thinking that determines the aging of your body, because thought influences the functions of the body. A negative pattern of thought can slow down or inhibit the action of any organ or process so that it shows evidence of what is termed old age.

The Body Is Always Young

A very interesting thing about the body is that the material which comprises it, the various atoms which constitute the cells that in turn make up the body structure, are being continually replaced. Various studies made by medical researchers indicate that at most no part of the body is over a year old. There is a continual process of new material being incorporated in and as the body and old material being discarded. From this point of view it is obvious that it is not the body itself which ages.

The Body's Pattern

That there is a pattern according to which the body conforms there is no doubt. There would have to be or else the food which you eat could never become the cells and structure of your body; no healing could take place, and no renewal could ever be effected. The Idea of body, the pattern, does not change. Neither does the Law through which it is projected into manifestation. So you find that both the primary cause and the means of its becoming tangible are timeless factors and universal in their effectiveness.

YOU CAN AVOID OLD AGE

What Grows Old?

The material which constitutes the body is constantly new; the manner in which it becomes the physical structure of the body is in accord with the great Law of Life which never lessens in Its action. At this point you find yourself confronted with the unique question: What does grow old? Not that there are not other factors involved, but the main thing which can influence the degree of aging that you experience is the process of your own thought. Theoretically, your body should not grow old, but you can and do permit your thinking about it to age, which is of course reflected in its functioning.

The Body Is a Mirror

Many a person at forty appears and acts as a person of eighty, and, on the other hand, you see a person at eighty who has more vitality than a person of forty. The source of such differences is found in the way the individual thinks. Many people feel that the age of fifty is the dividing line, that this is the point when old age starts. And of course the result is that at fifty they do enter old age. You seem to be as old or as young as you think you are. At most any point in life you can introduce into your body the evidences of old age by what you think about yourself. What counts is not what you see in the mirror, but what you mentally want to see in it!

A Better Picture

You need to establish a better mental picture of yourself, a picture of the way you want yourself to be, not of what you fear you will become. There is a natural process of maturing involved in all living things, but there is no reason why you should hasten or prematurely develop an advanced state of senility when you obviously should have many more years of happy living ahead of you. There is also the fact that you should ignore the evidence of statistics—that certain things happen to most people at certain ages. You are yourself, and not most people, and what happens to your body is directly related to what you think of yourself. There is no necessity for your physical condition to follow any statistical average.

YOU CAN AVOID OLD AGE

Does Thinking Age?

If it is your pattern of thinking that is largely responsible for the age you appear to be, then is there anything in the nature of thought itself which ages? Most evidence indicates that the ability to think does not age or deteriorate; rather, the contrary appears to be the case. Some research has indicated that there is an active maturity of thinking that can only be attained after fifty when most people are ready to give up and quit. There is also evidence that people who think in a creative and constructive manner live longer than others.

A Youthful Mind

The minute you cease being mentally alive, your body reflects this pattern of thought and begins to slow up and become sluggish in its action, and old age sets in. If you can train yourself to be active and productive in the way you think, and maintain a concept of a healthy, vital body, the body itself will readily conform to the pattern you have established for it. A youthful, active mind is your insurance against what others experience as old age.

MENTAL STIMULANTS

SCIENCE: *...I am sure we could still enormously lengthen the average human life-span by living in better harmony with natural laws.... We can do ourselves a great deal of good in this respect by just yielding to our natural cravings for variety in everyday life.*

—Hans Selye

PHILOSOPHY: *It is impossible to detach God from the world. God is the sustainer of body as well as its inner guide.*

—Sarvepalli Radhakrishnan

RELIGION: *...Behold, I make all things new.*

—Revelation 21:5

YOU CAN AVOID OLD AGE

THE DIET

Within the Mind of God and the action of the Law of Life there is nothing that can age. All the material substance which constitutes my body is ever available to it and the laws that govern my body's functioning never cease their action. Life knows what to do and how to do all that is needed for the full expression of Itself through me. I accept the action of Life as what I am, continually and vitally renewing and sustaining Itself. I no longer condemn myself by what I think to a present or approaching experience of old age. I now release all previous concepts of myself which have inhibited the normal, natural action of vital living. Mentally I keep myself alive, alert, and productive. The Mind of God never exhausts Itself. Its action as my mind is ever fresh, keen, and wholesome, and my body is a reflection of the nature of my thinking. I release my body from adherence to any negative thoughts I may have had about it, and leave it free to conform to the great Law of Life that continually renews it.

— Capsule Supplement —

I now determine that my thoughts shall contain nothing that is contrary to the vital and ever-new expression of Life in me. I discard all ideas of old age and affirm that my body is healthy, normal, and active.

❂   ❂   ❂

Today I will apply this idea to these aspects of my thoughts and actions:

_____

_____

My particular problem, condition, or situation which it can be used to correct is:

_____

_____

STOP BEING SICK

Ill-health Can Be a Habit

Just as some people are said to be accident-prone, that is, they are always having unfortunate things happen to them, so it is with others in relation to their health. They always seem to be sick, and not always with the same thing. These are the people who fill the doctors' offices. The medical man provides relief for one ailment only to find the patient back in a very short time with something else wrong with him. In spite of all that medical science does for him he insists on something being wrong. Illness can become a habit which will manifest itself in almost any part of the body.

Something Is Wrong '

This does not mean that the patient is not really ill. Sick he is, and something needs to be done about it. More often than not the patient is given medical assistance, then advised to change his habits, the way he lives, and his frame of mind. Along a similar line is the fact that regardless of how effective a medical treatment may be, there is little or nothing a doctor can do to save a person's life if the individual has no desire to live; the pattern of his thinking is wrong. And as to the manner in which he thinks, this is something that no one can do anything about except the person himself.

Escape from Illness

It is a well-known fact that a large number of individuals develop illness as an escape mechanism to keep from doing things they do not want to do, or to receive attention from

STOP BEING SICK

others that they feel they need. It is most difficult to deal with illness of this type until there is a change in the person's thinking. He will always find some illness to have. Actually such people need to learn to escape from illness, not to it!

Patterns of Experience

If your thinking embodies concepts of illness your body readily accommodates you by being ill. The reverse is also true: if you are healthy and desire to remain so, you will not entertain in any way the thought that illness is part of your experience. Illustrative of this are the almost miraculous recoveries of individuals who should by all rights have died. They wanted to be healthy and live. Conversely, individuals who encounter a minor illness often die when there is no medical reason for them to do so. To a larger degree than you might care to admit you alone appear to be responsible for the way your body is functioning.

Get Out of Your Way

As difficult as it may be, you often have to force yourself to get out of your own way so that Life can function normally and naturally within you. You can start to discard your aches and pains when you learn to so direct your thinking that it entertains ideas of health rather than illness. Left alone, the body can pretty well take care of itself, but if in ignorance you let your thinking behave in a wayward manner it causes nothing but grief. It had been indicated that illness, in approximately ninety-five per cent of the people, can be traced to mental and emotional causes.

Start To Get Well

If you are ill, or if you want to keep from getting ill, carefully and honestly examine your consistent way of thinking. There needs to be, literally, a mental housecleaning which discards all ideas that are opposed to a full, rich enjoyment of health. You need to create a new picture of yourself, a picture that contains the best that life has to offer in the way of health. Once you begin to see yourself in this manner, and accept health as your rightful state, then illness will have no sustaining cause in your thought.

STOP BEING SICK

Lack of Conflict

When you begin to create a pattern of health in your thinking, then your body has at least a good chance to be normal and healthy, and if medical attention is needed you will not be thwarting what medical science is doing for you. One of the most important things in discarding disease is to stop complaining about it, cease focusing your attention on it. What you give your attention to is augmented and promoted. As long as your thoughts dwell on illness you have little chance to escape from it, and you are in a running battle with Life which always seeks to express Itself in you in a normal, healthy manner. There is a need to mentally stop rejecting what you say you want.

Health Is an Inside Job

Regardless of the nature of the illness, the first step in getting rid of it starts with yourself. You need to have a will to live, a desire to be healthy. Such attitudes must be continually, not just occasionally maintained. Get out of the habit of entertaining thoughts to the contrary. When you are able to do this you automatically discard causative and sustaining patterns of thinking which for the most part have been responsible for your illness.

MENTAL STIMULANTS

SCIENCE: *It is the patient's faith that he is going to get better that is an important determining factor. He has to mentally accept health in order to experience it.*

—Alfred J. Cantor

PHILOSOPHY: *Thought and thing depend upon and correspond to each other.*

—Plotinus

RELIGION: *...put on the new man, which is renewed in knowledge after the image of him that created him.*

—Colossians 3:10

STOP BEING SICK

THE DIET

Life, which resides at the center of my being and is what I am, ever seeks to express Itself fully, normally, and naturally as healthy activity in my body. I no longer fight Its action within me, but accept all that It is. There is no illness in Life—God—and there is no necessity that I should experience illness. I let go of illness and accept health. I convince myself mentally and emotionally that health is mine to experience, and I accept it as my experience. I get my negative thinking out of the way, I cease entertaining concepts of myself as being other than healthy, and remove ideas which have nourished and sustained illness. My thinking is continually patterned after those ideas which are for my greatest good, and they are reflected in every cell, organ, and function of my body. Whatever needs to be done to re-establish my body's normal action is being done now, so that my body perfectly expresses the perfect pattern which is its source. All is well in God's world; this I accept as my physical experience, and all unlike it now ceases to be. I start to live Life, to experience a new surge of vigor and joy.

— Capsule Supplement —

I let the dynamic action of perfect Life flow freely and unobstructed through me. I no longer invite illness but declare that health alone is what I accept and experience.

❋　❋　❋

Today I will apply this idea to these aspects of my thoughts and actions:

_____

_____

My particular problem, condition, or situation which it can be used to correct is:

_____

_____

ENJOY NEW HEALTH
AND HAPPINESS

You Can't Have One Without the Other

Basically, health may be said to pertain to a state of the physical body, while, on the other hand, happiness refers to a state of mind. But you are both body and mind and cannot divide yourself into pieces. The body is not separate from the mind, nor the mind from the body. The condition of one is reflected in the other, although the mind can be said to be the dominant part—the part that is conscious, has volition, and is able to direct the action and activities of you as a whole.

The Key to Happiness

It appears that you cannot be happy unless you are healthy, and neither can you be healthy unless you are happy. This raises the question: If something is amiss, just where do you start to correct it? Do you start with the physical condition or the mental state that might be the causative factor? The answer, of course, is that you cannot deal with one part to the exclusion of the other. You do something about both mind and body at the same time by starting with the dominant aspect of your being, by paying attention to your thinking, for in your thinking rests the key to both physical well-being and mental health or happiness.

Learn To Be Normal

Both health and happiness can rightly be said to be your normal way of life. The body ever seeks to maintain itself in a state of health but too often your negative mental activity interferes with the process. As for your mind, happiness can be said to be the result of the feeling of joy and satisfaction which comes from constructive and creative effort. When

ENJOY NEW HEALTH AND HAPPINESS

you let your mind be constructive and creative, then you are letting it fulfill its purposive function and reason for existence, ever seeking to become a fuller expression of the Life that is within you.

Discard Unhappiness

A person who is unhappy because of lack of money can suddenly become happy as a result of an inheritance. But it is not the money itself that causes the change, rather it is a change in the way of thinking. Inheritance or no inheritance, you can create for yourself a pattern of thinking that is devoid of morbid and negative content. When you do this, and maintain such a pattern, you cannot avoid becoming more cheerful and happy. Unhappy patterns of thinking will indefinitely maintain themselves until you specifically and definitely replace them with constructive thoughts that will contribute to your well-being.

A Happy Body

Your body cannot possibly be healthy if it is constantly tortured and disrupted by negative thinking, unhappy thinking. If you permit yourself to be unhappy over a period of time, the body reflects this mental state and as a result you become additionally unhappy because your health is not what it should be. You have compounded your problem in a very unfavorable manner. Do all that is required physically to bring your body back to a normal state, but it will never stay that way unless you remove the irritating pattern of thinking that may have caused the trouble in the beginning.

A Happy Mind

A happy, healthy state of mind is more than just saying you are happy. It is not a case of ignoring conditions or situations about you which may contribute to such unhappiness, although this may be of some false benefit. The solution to the problem rests in mentally and physically engaging in constructive and creative endeavor. A happy mind is the one that is doing something worthwhile.

Happiness Starts Within You

As much as you may have relished being immersed in unhappiness, it is necessary

ENJOY NEW HEALTH AND HAPPINESS

that you recognize the sad state of your mental and physical affairs and the additional trouble you are headed for if you permit yourself to continue in such a manner. You have to impose a strict discipline on your way of thinking. This is not accomplished by wishful thinking, daydreaming, and hoping, but by definitely maintaining wholesome ideas which will manifest themselves as your experience of actual health and happiness. You can only experience that which is a reflection of the content of your mind.

The End of the Search

You may spend a lot of time hunting health and happiness but never seem able to catch up with them. What you desire you may seek to discover outside of yourself, little realizing that it is only within you that it can ever be found. What you want you already have, but you need to acknowledge this and act and think in a manner that permits you to accept and experience these things. When you become tired of an undesirable state of life, sell yourself some new ideas that contain more of what Life actually is.

MENTAL STIMULANTS

SCIENCE: *...health and happiness are not produced by situations or by other people; they are produced by one's own mind.*

— Curt S. Wachtel

PHILOSOPHY: *Place yourself in the middle of the stream of power and wisdom which flows into you as life, place yourself in the full center of that flood, then you are without effort impelled to truth, to right, and a perfect contentment.*

— Ralph Waldo Emerson

RELIGION: *Happy is the man that findeth wisdom, and the man that getteth understanding.*

— Proverbs 3:13

ENJOY NEW HEALTH AND HAPPINESS

THE DIET

It is in the nature of Life, Intelligence, God, that there is harmonious, joyous creative activity. That which I am in body and mind is an activity and expression of God and there is no necessity that I be other than healthy and happy. I recognize and accept the fact that physical well-being and mental satisfaction are mine to experience as I determine that they are mine. I direct my thinking into purposeful and constructive channels. As I eliminate all ideas to the contrary I free my body from the influence of disturbing and irritating mental factors. In spite of any unhappiness or mental depression I may now have, I am convinced that Life flows through me anew and re-establishes Itself in me in accord with Its true nature. In both mind and body I reflect my highest concept of the nature of God, who can do Himself no harm nor deprive Himself of the results of beneficial activity. I know that there is a Wisdom and a Power within me which now rightly guides me and directs me so that I continually enjoy a life that is worthwhile and experience health and happiness.

— Capsule Supplement —

Today and each day my life is an increasing experience and expression of health and happiness. I accept this as the normal activity of the Life that is within me.

✿   ✿   ✿

Today I will apply this idea to these aspects of my thoughts and actions:

_____

_____

My particular problem, condition, or situation which it can be used to correct is:

_____

_____

THE
LAST
TWO
DAYS

...of the mental diet offer concrete suggestions for the richer enjoyment of living and a practical approach to ways of attaining it.

DISCOVER A NEW JOY OF LIVING

YOU LIVE YOUR THOUGHTS

DISCOVER A NEW JOY OF LIVING

There Is Nothing You Can't Buy

Although they say the best things in life are free and you have discovered that there are some things money cannot buy, you also have found that nothing is really free. The universal coin of the realm with which you are dealing, the payments that must be made, can only be made with thoughts and ideas. Whether it is a tangible or intangible good that you wish to experience, the first and final payments can only be made by payments in thought.

Life Is Not a Bed of Roses

You need to remember that the life you live is not a continual bed of roses. There are problems to be met, difficulties to be overcome, things to be accomplished which require effort and sometimes sacrifice. But the joy that is to be gained in living is in properly meeting and mastering the inevitable vicissitudes of being alive. The difficulties that may confront you appear to be a necessary complement of life so that you can grow, accomplish, and achieve, and derive the satisfaction of having been of some value to yourself and others. To escape to a bed of roses would be avoidance of living—an existence which would be devoid of all meaning.

The Road Ahead

The road that you will travel through life is paved for you by the thoughts that you maintain today. Whether the road is smooth or rough depends on the harmonious or inharmonious, the constructive or destructive nature of your consistently maintained pattern of thinking. To have a better tomorrow depends first on mentally establishing it today.

DISCOVER A NEW JOY OF LIVING

In the Beginning

Every moment of your life is a new beginning. You cannot afford to wait until tomorrow to do that which you should do today. Every idea you have, every thought you think is in some way an initial causative factor which determines your experience. As long as you delay creating a mental concept of the good you desire, it is impossible for it to become part of your life. If you want to start to enjoy life more, the only time you can start is now; the more will never become your experience until you start to do something about it.

The Great Experiment

You guide your footsteps through life by your ability to think and imagine. You are faced with the continual challenge of so using your mind that it may contribute to your joy of living rather than deprive you of it. Your mind is your great laboratory wherein you may try experiment after experiment with definite results coming from each undertaking. You alone can determine what it is that you do there, and you cannot escape the consequences of what you do. Every thought you have, every experiment you undertake, can result in something beneficial going forth into creation in your experience.

Achievement

Once you embark on such a process of using your thought in a beneficial way you will discover that what you are doing is not of your own doing, but is rather the opening up of a greater channel for the fulfillment of the action and purpose of Life in and through you. You are letting Life be Itself as your life rather than attempting to stand alone and apart from It. The continual goal is to grow into a greater awareness of the nature of Life and a fuller acceptance of the good that It has to offer. You may progress in small steps or great leaps, but once you have learned to walk in this direction you will find every move will open up for you wider horizons of living.

Unlimited Funds

You have unlimited funds at your disposal for the purchase of all the good your heart desires. The funds are thoughts—creative causes in your mind. There is no limit to the

DISCOVER A NEW JOY OF LIVING

extent to which you may spend such funds, nor the manner in which you may spend them. However, you are always using them to buy something in your experience. What you purchase is up to you. But if it is a more joyous experience in living that you desire, be sure that the coins you use—the thoughts you maintain—are the right ones, for you cannot avoid receiving back that which is like them.

Refuse To Be Discouraged

"If at first you don't succeed, try, try again" may well apply at this point. You may find yourself seemingly defeated at every attempt to better your life. But you must remember that every idea of merit that you entertain adds to the sum total of the concept of good you want manifested in your experience. Keep at your endeavors and you will build up a balance in your favor so that a favorable outcome is inevitable.

MENTAL STIMULANTS

SCIENCE: *...the power and the will of the human mind is but a symptom of reality; that we, when we are most human, most rational, most aware of love and beauty, reflect and represent the spirit of the universe.*
—N. J. Berrill

PHILOSOPHY: *...there is something in each of us that merges with the Infinite and draws back into its own soul, mind, and experience as much of God as it comprehends.*
—Ernest Holmes

RELIGION: *...the fruit of the Spirit is love, joy, peace...gentleness, goodness, faith...against such there is no law.*
—Galatians 5:22-23

DISCOVER A NEW JOY OF LIVING

THE DIET

In all ways—in my acts, emotions, and thoughts—I more fully express the joyous nature of the Life that is at the center of my being. Joyous living now becomes my experience as I accept it as necessary and fundamental to a life that is a reflection of its Divine Source. I progress up the highway of life, idea by idea, experience by experience, and I pave my way only with those ideas which embody my greatest possible good. Regardless of how rough or discouraging the way may seem today, I know that tomorrow will be better because of the thoughts I establish today. I face life and living with joy in my heart, with enthusiasm in my mind, knowing that there is That within me which can and does express Itself through me in such a way that I continually grow, achieve, and mature into a better likeness of the Source which created me. I no longer delay or hinder my fuller enjoyment of living, but start now to establish it idea by idea, knowing that as each beneficial and constructive idea is established in my mind, it builds up to a point where, through the action of spiritual Law, it inevitably manifests as my experience. Joy, satisfaction, and continual achievement fill my life as a result of my knowing that God is an active partner with me in all my ways.

— Capsule Supplement —

Life is now a joyful adventure, for I know and accept the nature and action of the One Life flowing through me in all that I am and do.

✿ ✿ ✿

Today I will apply this idea to these aspects of my thoughts and actions:

_____

_____

My particular problem, condition, or situation which it can be used to correct is:

_____

_____

YOU LIVE YOUR THOUGHTS

You Always Experience Your Convictions

If there is one thing that you cannot do it is to be and experience other than what you maintain in the content of your thought. Regardless of what you may say you are convinced of, it is what you actually believe that will manifest itself. You may give lip service to certain ideas and professions of belief, but it is meaningless in comparison to the deep-seated emotional conviction you have relative to certain concepts basic to the nature of the life you are living. You may think that you can ignore your negative ways of thinking, but you are only kidding yourself. They will declare themselves in your life until you remove or replace them with ideas that are for your benefit.

Thirty Ideas

During this month you have encountered thirty ideas which can greatly influence the direction of your life. They are as old as man and as new as tomorrow's sunrise. There is nothing unusual or unique about them. But what can be new and unique is the manner in which you learn to recognize their value and use them in the practical matter of everyday living. Ideas are of no value unless they are applied and made to work. This is something that only you can do, no one else can do it for you. You think your own thoughts, but their creativeness of your experience rests in the nature of Life and Mind. Your only obligation is to think the right thoughts, the rest is automatically taken care of.

Use What You Know

No doubt there are many areas in your life which you would like to better. Perhaps some of the ideas you have encountered directly apply to them. In other cases it may

YOU LIVE YOUR THOUGHTS

require a combination of two or more of these ideas to properly deal with the situation you would like to correct. In using what you have come to know it must be remembered that the actual words in and of themselves have no value in respect to improving your life. Rather, the ideas that lie behind them is what is important. These ideas must be translated into your own terminology, into your own way of thinking. They have to be digested, assimilated, and made an integral part of your mental and emotional makeup. Then, and only then, can they become vital factors in creating and sustaining the good things you desire.

Life Is So Daily

Each and every day you are the living embodiment of your convictions. If you don't like what you appear to be it is time to provide yourself with a new set of convictions. This you can do; you have the foundations in the ideas you have encountered and there remains but to make them a practical part of your experience and not just idle theory. Every day you can in some way improve your convictions and see a tangible result. This is not a matter of idle thought, but rather is a sustained adherence to an idea which permits of nothing to the contrary. Not always easy, but it has been done, it is being done, and you can accomplish it in your life if you sincerely desire to do so.

Your Crystal Ball

As you move on from this into more and more thirty-day periods of your life it must be remembered that consistency is of the utmost importance. At the start of this thirty-day period you were instructed to devote time both morning and evening to the subject at hand. What could be more important in your life than allowing such special times for the benefit of all the other times of your day? There must be the doing on your part before there can be any results. The future can hold much more than you realize for you, for those you love, and those with whom you associate, if you start creating that future now. What happens tomorrow is but the lengthened shadow of thoughts you have today.

YOU LIVE YOUR THOUGHTS

Not a Serious Undertaking

You need to indulge in no serious self-analysis, no ponderous self-evaluation. You start simply and easily by just beginning to think in terms of what you desire rather than dwelling on what you do not want. Enjoy what you are doing, enter into the endeavor with enthusiasm and encouragement, firm in the knowledge and conviction that you are not responsible for the production of the results, they are effected through the action of the Spirit within you, Life Itself. Your responsibility is only in doing the proper thinking about yourself.

No Limit

There is no limit to the sphere of action of creative thought, just as there is no limit to the action of infinite Mind. In your world of experience your thought can be, and is, an effective factor in relation to any and every aspect of your health, affairs, and relationships. Do not be afraid to use it for any good thing. The more you use it in this manner the more you will be able to use it effectively. Man's greatest frontier lies in the discovery of the nature and power of his thought, and your most wonderful experiences of living lie ahead of you as you come to know and use the mind God has given you.

MENTAL STIMULANTS

SCIENCE: *...people will be happy when they have gained new knowledge and revere those things beyond science which really matter....*

                              —Werner Heisenberg

PHILOSOPHY: *So far as a man thinks, he is free.*

                              —Ralph Waldo Emerson

RELIGION: *...prove me now herewith, saith the Lord of hosts, if I will not open you the windows of heaven, and pour you out a blessing, that there shall not be room enough to receive it.*

                              —Malachi 3:10

YOU LIVE YOUR THOUGHTS

THE DIET

My life starts anew each day, each minute, and regardless of what the past may have been, or the present may be, I know that every instant is a new beginning. My future is determined by what I know, am convinced of, and have faith in, and there is That within me which guides and directs me in the acceptance of only the ideas which are for my greatest good. These ideas I recognize and retain, discarding all others, and it is out of these ideas that my tomorrows are born. My faith is proved constantly by what I am and what I experience. My conviction that the universe is a thing of law and order, and that in, through, and behind all things is the one Supreme Reality—God, Mind, Intelligence— now enables me to change and redirect the course of my life so that I experience a greater degree of all good things. The keys to the kingdom of good are my thoughts. I know how to use them properly for the benefit of myself and others, and I let nothing hinder or interfere with the constructive activity of my mind. This day and each day I use the creative power of my thought to establish a whole new world of worthwhile living. I continually prove to myself and to the world about me the strength and power of thoughts that reflect the nature of God.

— Capsule Supplement —

This day and every day I prove my conviction in a God that is good, and in His universe that is lawful and orderly. I believe that thoughts are things, that ideas become manifest, and my every experience is testimony to the rightness of what I believe.

❈　❈　❈

Today I will apply this idea to these aspects of my thoughts and actions:

_____

_____

My particular problem, condition, or situation which it can be used to correct is:

_____

_____

THIS
IS
MY
LIFE

The following pages are for your own use so that you may keep a record of what happens in your life. Many people have used and proved the value of such a procedure and you should avail yourself of its benefits.

First you enter the date on which you express your desire for an additional good in your experience. Then simply state the nature of it. Note references to the days of the 30-day Mental Diet which apply to it. Follow the same procedure as you have for each day of the mental diet, that is, morning and night use the diet for those days to firmly establish in your mind the conviction that that which you desire is now a part of your experience.

When it does come to be your actual experience, note the date and give thanks that it has been provided for you.

Now you are on your own. If the mental diet is followed consistently, you can see and experience every day the results of the diet of previous days. Don't deviate from your diet for it is the pathway to a richer, fuller way of living than you have yet dreamed of.

Date of entry _____

The good I desire to experience is: _____

_____

_____

The daily diets I will use to assist me are: _____

_____

Date of fulfillment _____

* * *

Date of entry _____

The good I desire to experience is: _____

_____

_____

The daily diets I will use to assist me are: _____

_____

Date of fulfillment _____

* * *

Date of entry _____

The good I desire to experience is: _____

_____

_____

The daily diets I will use to assist me are: _____

_____

Date of fulfillment _____

Date of entry _____

The good I desire to experience is: _____

_____

_____

The daily diets I will use to assist me are: _____

_____

Date of fulfillment _____

✿   ✿   ✿

Date of entry _____

The good I desire to experience is: _____

_____

_____

The daily diets I will use to assist me are: _____

_____

Date of fulfillment _____

✿   ✿   ✿

Date of entry _____

The good I desire to experience is: _____

_____

_____

The daily diets I will use to assist me are: _____

_____

Date of fulfillment _____